BUDDHISM, TAOISM AND OTHER FAR EASTERN RELIGIONS

Zondervan
Guide to Cults &
Religious Movements

Titles in the series released in 1995

Unmasking the Cults   *by Alan W. Gomes*
Jehovah's Witnesses   *by Robert M. Bowman, Jr.*
Masonic Lodge   *by George A. Mather and Larry A. Nichols*
Mormonism   *by Kurt Van Gorden*
New Age Movement   *by Ron Rhodes*
Satanism   *by Bob and Gretchen Passantino*
Unification Church   *by J. Isamu Yamamoto*
Mind Sciences   *by Todd Ehrenborg*

Titles in the series released in 1998

Astrology and Psychic Phenomena   *by André Kole and Terry Holley*
Buddhism, Taoism and Other Far Eastern Religions
   by J. Isamu Yamamoto
Goddess Worship, Witchcraft and Neo-Paganism   *by Craig S. Hawkins*
"Jesus Only" Churches   *by E. Calvin Beisner*
Hinduism, TM and Hare Krishna   *by J. Isamu Yamamoto*
Unitarian Universalism   *by Alan W. Gomes*
Truth and Error: Comparative Charts of Cults and Christianity
   by Alan W. Gomes

ZONDERVAN
GUIDE to CULTS &
RELIGIOUS
MOVEMENTS

BUDDHISM, TAOISM AND OTHER FAR EASTERN RELIGIONS

J. ISAMU YAMAMOTO
Author

Alan W. Gomes
Series Editor

ZondervanPublishingHouse
Grand Rapids, Michigan

A Division of HarperCollins*Publishers*

Dedicated to my wife, Barbara

Buddhism, Taoism and Other Far Eastern Religions
Copyright © 1998 by J. Isamu Yamamoto

Requests for information should be addressed to:
 Zondervan Publishing House
Grand Rapids, Michigan 49530

Library of Congress Cataloging-in-Publication Data

Yamamoto, J. Isamu.
    Buddhism, Taoism and other Far Eastern religions / J. Isamu Yamamoto.
       p.   cm. — (Zondervan guide to cults & religious movements)
    Includes bibliographical references.
    ISBN: 0-310-48912-1 (pbk.)
    1. East Asia—Religion. 2. Buddhism—Controversial literature. 3.
Christianity and other religions. I. Title. II. Series.
    BL1055.Y36   1998
    294.3—dc20
                                         95-52544
                                           CIP

Interior design by Art Jacobs

Printed in the United States of America

98 99 00 01 02 /❖ DP/ 10 9 8 7 6 5 4 3 2 1

 # Contents

How to Use This Book

The *Zondervan Guide to Cults and Religious Movements* comprises fifteen volumes, treating many of the most important groups and belief systems confronting the Christian church today. This series distills the most important facts about each and presents a well-reasoned, cogent Christian response. The authors in this series are highly qualified, well-respected professional Christian apologists with considerable expertise on their topics.

We have designed the structure and layout to help you find the information you need as quickly as possible. All the volumes are written in outline form, which allows us to pack substantial content into a short book. With some exceptions, each book contains, first, an introduction to the cult, movement, or belief system. The introduction gives a brief history of the group, its organizational structure, and vital statistics such as membership. Second, the theology section is arranged by doctrinal topic, such as God, Christ, sin, and salvation. The movement's position is set forth objectively, primarily from its own official writings. The group's teachings are then refuted point by point, followed by an affirmative presentation of what the Bible says about the doctrine. The third section is a discussion of witnessing tips. While each witnessing encounter must be handled individually and sensitively, this section provides some helpful general guidelines, including both dos and don'ts. The fourth section contains annotated bibliographies, listing works by the groups themselves and books written by Christians in response. Fifth, each book has a parallel comparison chart, with direct quotations from the group's literature in the left column and the biblical refutation on the right. Some of the books conclude with a glossary.

One potential problem with a detailed outline is that it is easy to lose one's place in the overall structure. Therefore, we have provided graphical "signposts" at the top of the odd-numbered pages. Functioning like a "you are here" map in a shopping mall, these graphics show your place in the outline, including the sections that come before and after your current position. (Those familiar with modern computer software will note immediately the resemblance to a "drop-down" menu bar, where the second-level choices vary depending on the currently selected main menu item.) In the theology section we have also used "icons" in the margins to make clear at a glance whether the material is being presented from the group's viewpoint or the Christian viewpoint. For example, in the Mormonism volume the sections presenting the Mormon position are indicated with a picture resembling the angel Moroni in the margin; the biblical view is shown by a drawing of the Bible.

We hope you will find these books useful as you seek "to give an answer to everyone who asks you to give the reason for the hope that you have" (1 Peter 3:15).

— Alan W. Gomes, Ph.D.
Series Editor

Part I: *Introduction*

I. Historical Background

A. Buddhism
1. Siddhartha Gautama, the Buddha[1]
   a. The problem of constructing an accurate biography
      (1) The first attempt at composing a formal biography of Siddhartha Gautama was probably at the end of the first century A.D., and it was entitled *Buddhacarita* by Asvaghosa.
      (2) Since the oral transmission of the accounts of Gautama's life occurred over several centuries, and since different Buddhist traditions hold to their own distinct version of his life, the trustworthiness of any biography of Gautama is subject to debate.
      (3) Moreover, many historians who do not profess to be Buddhists question whether any word about Gautama's life and teachings can be ascribed to him with unqualified certainty.
      (4) Nevertheless, because general agreement exists concerning the major incidents of Gautama's life and the primary tenets of his teachings among the Buddhist traditions, an account of his life and teachings can be presented with the assurance that most Buddhists will accept at least the basic outline of the following account.
   b. Early life
      (1) Siddhartha Gautama was born about 560 B.C. in Kapilavastu in southern Nepal.
      (2) Since his father was a chieftain of the Sakya clan, Gautama grew up enjoying a life of luxury as a prince. In fact, his father secluded him from observing any human misery.
      (3) One fateful day, however, Gautama eluded the royal attendants and drove his chariot outside his father's palace and witnessed the effects of human suffering when he saw an old man, a leper, a corpse, and an ascetic.
      (4) Thus Gautama realized that worldly happiness was an illusion.

---

[1]My primary source for the biography of Siddhartha Gautama is Edward J. Thomas, *The Life of Buddha as Legend and History* (London: Routledge & Kegan Paul, 1969). Many scholars in the Buddhist field consider this book the best on the subject.

c. His pilgrimage
   (1) After Gautama's son, Rahula, was born, Gautama renounced his worldly life and pursued his quest for truth as a wandering monk.
   (2) For six or seven years, Gautama practiced many forms of extreme austerity in order to attain truth, such as sleeping on brambles to mortify the desires of his body and abstaining from sitting by crouching on his heels to develop his concentration.
   (3) Finally, Gautama realized that his life as an ascetic was of no greater value than his previous life as a prince. Indeed, self-torture was vain and fruitless, just as a life full of worldly pleasure.
   (4) After Gautama understood the importance of the Middle Way, he abandoned his life of extreme austerities.
d. The Enlightened One
   (1) Later at Gaya, Gautama sat at the foot of a particular fig tree, which is commemorated as the Bodhi-tree.
   (2) Gautama meditated there until he became enlightened, discovering the Four Noble Truths, which became the central tenets of his teachings and of Buddhist philosophy. (The Four Noble Truths will be explained and examined in detail under "Part II: Theology.")
   (3) At this point in Gautama's spiritual odyssey, he became the Buddha, which means "the Enlightened One."
e. The Buddha's mission
   (1) After his enlightenment, instead of withdrawing from all human contact with the knowledge he had gained, as other holy men had done, the Buddha decided to share the Four Noble Truths with all who would receive his teachings.
      (a) This decision symbolized the compassion of the Buddha—his unselfish concern for others.
      (b) Thus the Buddha established the Buddhist faith both on his wisdom and compassion.
   (2) Two months after his enlightenment, the Buddha gave his first sermon in the Deer Park at Rishipatana. This event set in motion what Buddhists call the Wheel of the Law (i.e., stages in comprehending ultimate reality).
   (3) Subsequently, people began to follow the Buddha, who received them into the Sangha, the Buddhist community of beggar-monks.
   (4) The Buddha was the teacher and spiritual guide for his followers, but he did not demand submission to him as their leader nor did he require a vow of obedience to himself.

(5) For more than forty years the Buddha dedicated himself to his ministry until his death at the age of about eighty.

2. Early Buddhism[2]

  a. Sangha

    (1) After the Buddha passed away, his followers continued to wander from village to village, spreading the Buddha's doctrine of deliverance from suffering.

    (2) As the Sangha grew, the Buddhist monks separated from one another, forming numerous groups with each interpreting the Buddha's teachings differently from one another.

    (3) During the rainy seasons, wealthy landowners would provide shelters for many of these groups of monks.

      (a) In time one group after another accepted the patronage of various landowners, establishing monasteries throughout India.

      (b) Thus the Sangha eventually evolved from a society of wandering monks and nuns to a community of Buddhist monasteries.

    (4) After conquering most of India, King Asoka embraced Buddhism in the middle of the third century B.C.

      (a) Buddhism was at the height of its acceptance in India under this monarch.

      (b) King Asoka also vigorously promoted a campaign to spread Buddhist doctrine throughout Asia and the Near East.

      (c) It was during this time that Buddhism became a world religion.

  b. Dharma (i.e., the doctrine expounded by the Buddha)

    (1) Since a systematic Buddhist theology was not put into written form apparently until four centuries after the Buddha's death, schisms split the Sangha because Buddhists within different monasteries argued over the content of the Buddha's teachings.

      (a) The word *dharma* has a variety of meanings in the context of Indian culture.

      (b) In Buddhism the Dharma is the truth taught by the Buddha.

    (2) By the close of the third century B.C., the Buddhists were separated into no less than eighteen major schools.

    (3) Two major branches of Buddhism eventually developed: Theravada ("the doctrine of the elders") and Mahayana ("the Great Wheel").

---

[2]An exhaustive discussion of the early Sangha and the Dharma appears in Edward Conze, I. B. Horner, and David Snellgrove, eds., *Buddhist Texts through the Ages* (New York: Harper & Row, 1964).

3. Theravada Buddhism[3]

  a. Theravada Buddhism is said to be the fundamentalist branch of Buddhism because it has preserved most of the original nature of Buddhism.

  b. By the first century B.C., Buddhist scriptures were collected and written in the Pali language, a vernacular that descended from Indian Sanskrit.

   (1) These scriptures became known as the Pali Canon and provided the foundation for Theravada beliefs and practices.

   (2) The Theravadins believe that the Pali Canon is an accurate account of what the Buddha taught.

  c. Theravada Buddhism contains major points of doctrine that differ from the beliefs of most Mahayana schools.

   (1) Most significantly, the Theravadins revere the Buddha as a great ethical teacher, but not as a god as many of the Mahayanists do.

   (2) The Theravadins reserve their teachings for the Buddhist saints (arhants) and not for the common people, which is another departure from many of the Mahayana schools.

   (3) According to the Theravadins, only the Buddhist saints can attain ultimate deliverance (nirvana), while many Mahayanists believe that bodhisattvas—beings who have achieved enlightenment but delay nirvana for themselves—can save others through their accumulated merits.

  d. Buddhaghosa is unquestionably the foremost commentator of Theravada Buddhism.

   (1) Buddhaghosa was born in the latter half of the fourth century A.D. into a Brahman family, but converted to Buddhism.

   (2) In Sri Lanka, Buddhaghosa compiled an extensive encyclopedia of Pali Buddhist literature that retains its authority today.

   (3) Theravadins regard Buddhaghosa as the greatest scholar of their religion.

  e. Like the other schools of Buddhism, Theravada Buddhism suffered severe persecution at the hands of Hindus and Moslems, who finally removed most of Buddhism from India—the land of its birth—by the thirteenth century.

   (1) Today, Theravada Buddhism primarily thrives in Sri Lanka, while experiencing a resurgence in other parts of Southeast Asia outside of India.

---

[3]The classical discussion of the development of early Buddhist philosophy as it developed into various schools—Theravada, Mahayana, Madhyamika, and Yogacara in particular—is articulated in David J. Kalupahana, *Buddhist Philosophy: A Historical Analysis* (Honolulu: The University Press of Hawaii, 1976).

(2) Although Theravada Buddhism has suffered because of the opposition of other religions and of communism, it enjoys a friendly relationship with the other branches of Buddhism.

(3) The spread of Theravada teachings to the West has been limited to a small number of Westerners.

(4) With the large migration of Cambodians, Laotians, and other Southeast Asians, Theravada Buddhism now has a strong following in North America in such cities as Los Angeles and Seattle.

4. Mahayana Buddhism

  a. Mahayana Buddhism probably emerged in reaction against the severe austerity and individualism of early Buddhism.

  b. Whereas the Theravadins emphasized strenuous ascetic discipline for the elite few, the Mahayanists taught that everyone can have faith in and devotion for the Buddha and love and compassion for all living beings.

  c. The Theravadins believe that nirvana is achieved by eradicating one's own misery and karma through self-denial, but the Mahayanists argue that nirvana is attained by the realization that the essence of suffering and all that cause suffering (karma) is empty or void (*sunya*).

  d. Theravada Buddhism is sometimes said to be the Southern School of Buddhism, because it is predominant in Southeast Asia. Meanwhile, Mahayana Buddhism is sometimes regarded to be the Northern School of Buddhism, because it is dominant in Tibet, Mongolia, China, Korea, and Japan.

5. Mahayana: Madhyamika School

  a. In the late second century A.D., the Buddhist philosopher Nagarjuna founded the Madhyamika school, or the School of the Middle Path.

    (1) According to some accounts, Nagarjuna was trained as a Brahmin in South India, but he converted to Mahayana Buddhism.

    (2) Crucial to the development of Buddhist philosophy, Nagarjuna refined the doctrines that all existing things are "empty" (*sunya*) and that the Buddhist ideal is nonattachment to any idea, emotion, behavior, or physical entity.

    (3) Many Buddhist schools acknowledge him as a patriarch; indeed, Tibetan and other East Asian Buddhists revere him as a bodhisattva (i.e., a being who seeks enlightenment but delays Buddhahood in order to save others first with his own merits).

    (4) Nagarjuna accomplished the second turn of the Wheel of the Law (the second stage in comprehending ultimate reality), the Buddha having fulfilled the first.

11

    b. As a philosophical school, Madhyamika was established in China in the fifth century A.D. and Tibet in the eighth century A.D.

    c. Eventually Madhyamika died out as an independent school. Nevertheless, its doctrine on emptiness continued to strongly influence all Mahayana thought.

6. Mahayana: Yogacara School

    a. Two brothers, Asanga and Vasubandhu, founded the Yogacara school of Mahayana Buddhism in India during the fourth or fifth century A.D.

      (1) They contended that the world exists only in the mind of the perceiver.

      (2) They taught that only the mind or consciousness is real.

      (3) Some Buddhists believe that they established the third turn of the Wheel of the Law; that is, they took Buddhist philosophy to a higher level.

    b. Yogacara means the "practice of yoga."

      (1) While the Madhyamikas did not focus on yoga, the Yogacarins stressed it.

      (2) The Yogacarins maintained that the intense practice of meditative yoga results in the realization of the Absolute, which is nondual and nonconceptual, transcending worldly experience, "where there is undiscriminated consciousness without subject-object dichotomy."[4]

7. Mahayana in China

    a. Buddhism made serious inroads into China during the Han dynasty,[5] probably in the first century A.D.

      (1) Buddhism initially received a hostile reception in China, where many Chinese considered Buddhism a barbarous, foreign doctrine.

      (2) The Chinese have a high regard for the family and a deep appreciation for nature. Both of these values conflicted with the concept of detachment crucial to Buddhist philosophy.

      (3) Nevertheless, Buddhism was able to root firmly into Chinese culture under the patronage of the Tartar kings from the third to the sixth century A.D.

      (4) Although Buddhism was an adopted child, the Chinese eventually came to regard Chinese Buddhism as one of their own.

    b. The major schools of Mahayana Buddhism in China are T'ien-t'ai, Hua-yen, Ch'an, and the Pure Land sects.

---

[4]Ibid., 143.
[5]The Han dynasty existed from 202 B.C. to A.D. 220.

8. Mahayana in Tibet and Mongolia[6]
   a. During the reign of Songtsen Gampo in the seventh century, Buddhism secured a permanent place in the religious life of Tibet.
      (1) Songsten Gampo built Buddhist temples in Tibet.
      (2) He sent Tibetan scholars to other countries to study Buddhism and also invited Buddhist teachers to his country.
      (3) He also moved his capital from Yarlung to Lhasa ("God's place"), which became the center for Tibetan Buddhism.
   b. Padma-Sambhava brought Tantric Buddhism from India to Tibet.
      (1) Trisong Detsen succeeded Songtsen Gampo to the Tibetan throne and continued to invite Buddhist masters to Tibet, including Padma-Sambhava in 747.
      (2) The Tantras, which Padma-Sambhava taught, were esoteric Indian writings that emphasized mystical and occultic practices to achieve quick enlightenment.
      (3) The Tibetans quickly adopted the teachings of this sorcerer, Padma-Sambhava, whom they revere as the second Buddha.
      (4) The syncretism of the Tibetan ancient religion of Bon (animistic shamanism), the doctrines of Mahayana Buddhism (especially of Nagarjuna), and the tantric practices of Padma-Sambhava eventually formed Tibetan Buddhism.
   c. Some Buddhists view Tibetan Buddhism as a separate branch of Buddhism because it is distinct from Theravada and Mahayana Buddhism in many ways.
      (1) As a separate branch or vehicle, it is known as Vajrayana Buddhism or the "Diamond Vehicle" of Buddhism.
      (2) The key figure in Tibetan Buddhism is the priest-teacher known as the *lama* ("wisdom"), which is why this form of Buddhism is also known as "Lamaism."
      (3) The four major orders of Tibetan Buddhism are the Nyingmapa, the Kargyupa, the Saskyapa, and the Gelugpa.
   d. The Dalai Lama is the spiritual leader of Tibetan Buddhism.
      (1) *Dalai* is a Mongolian word that means "ocean"; thus, the rendering of Dalai Lama is "ocean of wisdom."
      (2) In 1950, Tenzin Gyatso was installed as the fourteenth Dalai Lama, and currently lives in exile because Tibet is still under the domination of communist China.
      (3) The Dalai Lama is an international ambassador of the Tibetan people and a symbol of their religious tradition.

---

[6]An excellent discussion of the history of Tibetan Buddhism is detailed in David Snellgrove and Hugh Richardson, *A Cultural History of Tibet* (Boulder, Colo.: Prajna Press, 1980).

e. Kublai Khan declared the Tibetan form of Buddhism as the national religion of Mongolia in the thirteenth century.

   (1) Even after the collapse of the Mongol dynasty, Tibetan Buddhism flourished in Mongolia until the communist government instituted an antireligious campaign against Buddhism from 1937 to 1939.

   (2) As nationalism has revived in Mongolia with the decline of communism and the withdrawal of Soviet troops in the early 1990s, Tibetan Buddhism has also experienced a resurgence in Mongolia.

9. Mahayana in Korea and Japan[7]

   a. Sunto, a Chinese monk, brought Buddhism to Korea in A.D. 372.

      (1) One of the three Korean kingdoms built the first Buddhist temples in 375.

      (2) After Korea was unified in the seventh century, the golden age of Buddhist art and literature in Korea endured until the fifteenth century.

      (3) During the Yi dynasty (1392–1910), Buddhism declined in Korea because of the antipathy of the Korean rulers toward Buddhism, while Confucianism flourished.

      (4) The most vibrant form of Buddhism in South Korea today is Won ("complete") Buddhism.

   b. Korean monks introduced Buddhism to Japan in 538, bringing Buddhist texts and icons with them.

      (1) In 593 Prince Shotoku vigorously supported Buddhism by establishing Buddhist monasteries in Japan.

      (2) Later manifestations of Buddhism in Japan had their origins in China.

      (3) The earliest forms of Buddhism, known as the six Nara Buddhist schools, were the Kusha, the Jojitsu, the Sanron, the Hosso, the Kegon, and the Ritsu.

         (a) They were officially supported, and they predominated in the eighth century.

         (b) Their traditions were mainly observed and studied in the Japanese academic community.

      (4) During the Heian period (794–1185), the first two major schools of Japanese Buddhism emerged.

         (a) Saicho (767–822) studied T'ien-T'ai in China and developed it in Japan as Tendai Buddhism, which taught the synthesis of meditation and moral purity.

---

[7]For a comprehensive analysis of the origin and development of all the important schools of Japanese Buddhism, see E. Dale Saunders, *Buddhism in Japan with an Outline of Its Origins in India* (Philadelphia: University of Pennsylvania Press, 1971).

    (b) Kukai (774–835) studied Chen-yen in China and developed it in Japan as Shingon Buddhism, which stressed esoteric elements of Tantric Buddhism.

    (c) Both Tendai and Shingon currently have a large following in Japan, while a minority of Japanese Americans belong to either of these religions.

10. Mahayana: Amida Buddhism

  a. The Amida Buddha

    (1) According to Buddhist tradition, millions of ages ago Dharmakara, a Buddhist monk, became the Amida Buddha because of his innumerable good deeds and great wisdom.

    (2) He then purified a land—a paradise where good Buddhists go after they have died. It is called the Pure Land.

    (3) Beings stay in the Pure Land until they attain nirvana (i.e., extinction).

  b. In 1175, Honen (1133–1212) established the Jodo sect (School of the Pure Land).

    (1) Honen taught a gentle and simple faith in the Amida Buddha.

    (2) He believed the formula *Namu Amida Butsu* (or *Nembutsu*) assures salvation—that is, entry into the Pure Land at death—to those who are sincerely devoted to the Amida Buddha.

    (3) He also said that faith in the compassion of the Amida Buddha would bring true happiness to believers.

  c. Shinran Shonin (1173–1262) founded the Jodo-Shinshu (True School of the Pure Land).

    (1) Shonin was Honen's most important disciple.

    (2) He taught that a Buddhist believer can be saved only by faith in the Amida Buddha.

    (3) He held that anyone who accepts the Amida Buddha as his or her savior would be admitted into the Pure Land.

  d. The Pure Land schools of Buddhism are important primarily in Japan and Korea.

    (1) In fact, more Japanese Buddhists are in the Pure Land schools than in any other Buddhist sects.

    (2) In addition, a majority of Japanese-American Buddhists belong to one of the Pure Land schools—primarily Jodo-Shinshu.

11. Mahayana: Zen Buddhism

  a. Zen is a meditation discipline whose primary goal is to experience enlightenment through meditation (*satori*).

    (1) Zen is the Japanese pronunciation of the Chinese *Ch'an,* an abbreviation of *Chan-na.*

    (2) *Chan-na* is the Chinese rendering of the Indian Sanskrit word *Dhyana,* which means meditation.

      (3) Over the centuries a highly refined form of meditation evolved as it migrated from India to China and Korea and finally to Japan.

    b. In 1191 Myoan Eisai (1141–1215) brought the Lin-chi (Rinzai) school of Zen Buddhism to Japan from China.

      (1) He was primarily responsible for the introduction of Zen as an independent Buddhist school in Japan.

      (2) Zen ideas had been present in the Tendai and Shingon Japanese sects, which vigorously opposed Eisai.

      (3) After receiving protection from Minamoto Yoriie (1182–1204), the shogun (i.e., the military leader of Japan), Eisai altered matters of doctrine and practice to fit in with the samurai philosophy.

    c. Dogen (1200–1253) was the founder of the Soto school of Zen Buddhism.

      (1) Like Eisai, Dogen studied and practiced Buddhist meditation in China before bringing what he learned back to Japan.

      (2) Unlike Eisai, Dogen refused to mix any other ideas or concepts with Zen.

      (3) He taught that enlightenment is achieved through continuous effort at reaching deeper levels of awareness, and not a quick experience stimulated by a flash of understanding during meditation as Eisai believed.

      (4) Dogen established the first independent Zen monastery in Japan.

    d. Zen is one of the most appealing forms of Buddhism to non-Asian Westerners.

      (1) Zen master Soyen Shaku's appearance at the World Parliament of Religions at the Chicago World's Fair of 1893 was significant in making North Americans aware of Zen Buddhism.

      (2) The works and proselytizing of D. T. Suzuki, another Japanese Zen master, were instrumental in popularizing Zen in North America.

      (3) Furthermore, "Zen has found especially friendly reception in the West among psychotherapists, poets, and artists."[8]

12. Mahayana: Nichiren Buddhism

    a. Zennichimaro[9] (1222–1282) founded Nichiren Buddhism.

      (1) Zennichimaro studied at the temples of the Tendai, Jodo, Zen, and Shingon schools of Buddhism in Japan.

---

[8]C. W. Edwards, "Zen," in *The Perennial Dictionary of World Religions,* ed. Keith Crim (San Francisco: Harper & Row, 1989), 825.

[9]At this time most Japanese commoners had no family name.

(2) As a Buddhist priest, he came to the belief that the *Lotus Sutra* contained the supreme teachings of the Buddha.

(3) He assumed the name Nichiren, which means "sun lotus," the "sun" referring to Japan and "lotus" to the *Lotus Sutra*.

(4) He taught that enlightenment is available to any person who faithfully and devotedly chants the prayer of praise (*Daimoku*) to the *Lotus Sutra: "Namu myo-ho-renge-kyo"* (i.e., "Hail to the wonderful truth of the Lotus Sutra").

(5) In addition, Nichiren condemned the other Buddhist schools. In fact, he once said, "The Nembutsu—Amida Buddhism—is hell; Zen is a devil; Shingon is the nation's ruin; and Ritsu is treason."[10]

(6) Because of his unrelenting campaign against the religious and political establishments of his time, he was arrested and exiled to a remote island in the Japan Seas, where he instituted the worship of the *Gohonzon*.

    (a) The *Gohonzon* is a small altar that houses a piece of paper used as a *mandala* (a visual object upon which to meditate).

    (b) This paper contains the words to their sacred chant.

b. After Amida Buddhism, Nichiren Buddhism presently has the largest number of Buddhist followers in Japan.

(1) Nineteen major Nichiren sects currently are active in Japan.

(2) All of those Nichiren schools revere the *Lotus Sutra,* exalt the worship of the *Gohonzon,* and honor Nichiren as the incarnation of Jogyo, a bodhisattva (Buddhist god).

(3) They also claim that Nichiren Buddhism represents the only true Buddhism, and they are especially hostile to Christianity.

c. The Soka Gakkai is a lay Nichiren Buddhist movement.

(1) The Soka Gakkai was founded in 1930 to promote one of the Nichiren sects, namely, Nichiren Shoshu.

(2) Enormously successful, it has gained over 17 million converts in over 117 nations.[11]

(3) Moreover, the Soka Gakkai has the third largest political party—the Komeito—in Japan.

(4) Recently, its connection with Nichiren Shoshu has been severely strained. It appears that the priests in Nichiren Shoshu are jealous of the prosperity enjoyed by the Soka Gakkai.

(5) The appeal of the Soka Gakkai in the West is largely due to its emphasis on the promise of materialistic gain and personal power.

---

[10]N. S. Brannen, "Nichiren Buddhism," in *The Perennial Dictionary of World Religions,* 538.

[11]William M. Alnor, "Name It and Claim It Style of Buddhism Called America's Fastest Growing Religion," *Christian Research Journal* (Winter/Spring 1989): 26.

B. Taoism

1. Simply said, *Tao* (pronounced "dao") means "the way."
   a. Actually, the *Tao* cannot truly be expressed in words. In fact, since the *Tao* cannot be defined, attempts to express it have resulted in many different meanings.
   b. For example, Taoist philosophers spoke of the *Tao* in metaphysical terms as the source and essence of Absolute Reality.
   c. Meanwhile, Confucius referred to the *Tao* as an ethical concept, a way of behaving.
2. Historians still debate the emergence of Taoism in China.
   a. The idea of *Tao* existed long before the Taoists established themselves as an organized religion, perhaps dating back as far as the seventh century B.C.
   b. According to some traditional Taoists, Lao Tzu ("Old Master") established the Taoist religion when he wrote *Lao Tzu* (later called *Tao-Te Ching*—"the way and its power") in the sixth century B.C.
   c. Most scholars, however, consider Lao Tzu as a legendary figure and the *Tao-Te Ching* as an anthology of sayings by many people, collected and edited between 350–275 B.C.
3. Taoism has evolved into philosophical and religious Taoism.
   a. Although both groups belong to a common tradition, some of their characteristics conflict.
   b. Philosophical Taoism is seen as rational, contemplative, and nonsectarian, viewing death as a natural occurrence when one returns to the *Tao*.
   c. Religious Taoism is seen as magical, cultic, esoteric, and sectarian, utilizing the occult to attain physical immortality.
4. Taoism exists today in many countries throughout the world.
   a. The Taoist tradition is active in Singapore, Indonesia, Thailand, Hong Kong, Hawaii, and particularly Taiwan.
   b. Because of the antireligious campaign of the communists, few pure Taoists currently practice their religion in China.
      (1) The Chinese communist government has allowed only a few select Taoist temples to function in China as historical relics of the past.
      (2) Nevertheless, Taoist concepts still influence many of the Chinese people.
      (3) In the past decade Taoist ideas are beginning to be openly expressed.
   c. Taoist concepts and icons have also become increasingly visible in North America.

C. Confucianism

1. The life of Confucius (551–449 B.C.)[12]

   a. Confucius is the latinized form of K'ung Fu-Tzu, which means "Great Master K'ung."

   b. Confucius was born in present-day Shantung.

   c. Although from a lineage of nobility, his family apparently was poor, which accounts for Confucius providing for his own education.

   d. After a successful career as a government official, Confucius became a political reformist in his fifties, eventually attracting thousands of followers.

   e. Nevertheless, during his lifetime Confucius never received the veneration of the Chinese people. In fact the Chinese rulers of various states either ignored or banished him.

   f. Confucius fought ceaselessly to reform the political corruption of his day. While on his deathbed, however, he regarded himself as a failure since he did not live to see the effects of his teachings on Chinese society.

2. The teachings of Confucius

   a. After observing the tragic consequences of civil wars between various Chinese states, sanctioned oppression of the people by state rulers, and widespread immorality within his society, Confucius preached a moral code based on benevolence toward others.

   b. Confucius argued that when people, and especially rulers, behave with "reciprocity" (*shu*), peace and order would be restored to the world. Confucius described *shu* as "not doing to others what you would not have them do to you."[13]

   c. Confucius believed that the social environment was a result of the character of the ruler and that the condition molded the individual. Thus Confucius taught that if a ruler is good and just, the people will be virtuous and obedient, and that if the ruler is cruel and exacting, the people will be rebellious and self-centered.

   d. Confucius also changed the meaning of *chun tzu,* "the Chinese gentlemen." Before Confucius, *chun tzu* had denoted "a man of good birth, whose ancestors had belonged to a stratum above that of the common herd. ... Confucius, on the contrary, asserted that any man might be a gentleman, if his conduct were noble, unselfish, just, and kind."[14]

---

[12]Most of what we know of Confucius can be found in the *Analects* and the *Mencius,* writings of his later followers and included in the Confucian canon.

[13]*Analects* V, 11; XV, 23.

[14]H. G. Creel, *Chinese Thought from Confucius to Mao Tse-tung* (New York: Mentor, 1953), 30–31.

3. The development of Confucianism
  a. During the early history of Confucianism, Mencius and Hsun Tzu emerged as the great teachers of Confucianism.
    (1) Mencius believed that human nature is inherently good and that people have a duty to cultivate that goodness in order to bring social harmony to the world.
    (2) On the other hand, Hsun Tzu taught that human nature is basically evil and that social restraints need to be placed upon people to control those evil tendencies.
    (3) Both schools of thought taught that perfectibility of the individual can be achieved through education and virtuous conduct.
  b. During the Han dynasty (206 B.C.–A.D. 220), Confucianism officially became the state religion.
    (1) A Confucian canon was established, which included the Five Classics and the Four Books. The *I Ching* (the Book of Changes) is one of the Classics and is a handbook on divination.
    (2) Also, the cult of Confucius emerged as part of the state religion, in which offerings were even sacrificed to Confucius at Confucian temples.
  c. Neo-Confucianism followed during the Sung dynasty (960–1279).
    (1) Some exchange of ideas had occurred among Confucianism, Buddhism, and Taoism.
    (2) In addition, Confucianism had somewhat softened its ethical code as a state religion.
    (3) Thus a Neo-Confucian revival marked a return to the fundamental ethical teachings of the early tradition of Confucianism.
  d. Confucianism is still influential, particularly among the Chinese.
    (1) Although the communists have persistently continued their hostility toward the teachings of Confucius, his ethics still play a significant role in the lives of many Chinese.
    (2) Outside of the influence of communism, people of Chinese background still venerate Confucius and his teachings.
    (3) Among non-Asians Confucian influence has been minimal in the West.

D. **Bon**
  1. Bon influence
    a. Despite not being able to fully determine the meaning of its name and its origin, we do know that Bon is a shamanistic religion whose presence in Tibet long preceded Buddhism.

    b. Although Bon was the major belief of the ancient Tibetans, Tibetan Buddhism developed from elements in Bon and Buddhism, which was introduced into Tibet in the mid-eighth century. This development caused Bon to recede in importance within Tibetan culture as a popular religion.

    c. As an animistic religion, it still dominates the beliefs of tribal cults in the isolated, rural regions of northern and western Tibet.

  2. Bon cosmology

    a. Adherents of Bon believe that the first king of Tibet was a son of the "King of Heaven," who ruled the cosmos along with his divine attendants.

    b. At that time heavenly and earthly beings could travel between their two worlds by means of a ladder, but later black magic cut the ladder, and access to the King of Heaven ceased.

    c. Only a handful of powerful shamans can hope to grasp the "spirit rope" and ascend to the highest heaven.

    d. The gShen-rabs is traditionally believed to be the founder of the Bon religion and the archetype of all Bon shamans.

    e. These Bon shamans use magic to heal and control the spirit beings who can be either good gods or evil goblins.

    f. These spirit beings "are rooted in nature and reflect the capricious and violent forces of nature that render life in Tibet precarious."[15]

E. Shinto

  1. Its name

    a. Until about the fourth or fifth century, the Shinto religion in Japan was apparently nameless.

    b. At that time it received the name *Shinto,* which means "way of the gods (*kami*)."

    c. Shinto is derived from the Chinese *shen-tao;* the "–to" of Shinto came from the Chinese *tao,* "the way."

    d. Historian John B. Noss points out, "Cultured Japanese in ancient times often borrowed Chinese words, as being more distinguished. In pure Japanese, the word is *kami-no-michi,* which has the same meaning."[16]

  2. Its development

    a. A few centuries before Christ, Shinto ideas and rituals emerged among different religious traditions from various parts of ancient Japan.

    b. Japanese priests collected many local traditions and unified them into a religion that became central to Japan's national heritage.

---

[15]D. G. Dawe, "Bon," in *The Perennial Dictionary of World Religions,* 114.

[16]John B. Noss, *Man's Religions,* 2d ed. (New York: Macmillan, 1956), 400.

    c. The result was the Shinto religion, which dominated the religious life of the Japanese until Buddhism was introduced to Japan about A.D. 500.

    d. Since Shinto lacked a systematic dogma of its own, Buddhism complemented it well, and though there has been some conflict between the two religions, for the most part they have coexisted well in Japan.

    e. After World War II, Japan evolved from an agricultural way of life into an industrial society, which has lessened Japanese interest in Shinto's rituals pertaining to the forces of nature.

    f. Nevertheless, the concepts of ancestor veneration, family loyalty, social cooperation, and, to a lesser extent, emperor worship still continue in the religious fabric of Japanese culture.

3. Its cosmology

    a. According to Shinto teachings, Izanagi and Izanami, who represent the male and female cosmic forces similar to the Yin and Yang of Taoism, created Amaterasu Omikami, the Sun Goddess.

    b. The Japanese worshiped Amaterasu at the Grand Imperial Shrine at Ise until 1945.

    c. Adherents of Shinto believe all the Japanese emperors, including the current Emperor Akihito, are descendants of Amaterasu Omikami.

    d. Thus the imperial line has been the focus of Japanese worship throughout most of Japanese history, although they have functioned as figureheads and not as rulers for the past millennium.

4. Kami

    a. A characteristic feature of Shinto is the belief in the kami (i.e., local deities), which pervades all of Japanese culture.

    b. Whereas the Buddhists erected temples for places of worship in Japan, Shinto priests built shrines in connection with the kami.

    c. Magical formulas and incantations are prevalent in Shinto as a way to call upon the kami to increase harvests, bless one's family, and ward off misfortunes.

II. Vital Statistics

A. *Estimated Figures*[17]

1. Buddhists

    a. 314, 939,000 worldwide

    b. 313,114,000 in Asia

---

[17]*Statistical Abstract of the United States: 1993,* 113th ed. (Washington, D.C.: U.S. Bureau of the Census, 1993), 69.

   c. 558,000 in North America
2. Confucians
   a. 6,028,000 worldwide
   b. 5,994,000 in Asia
   c. 26,000 in North America
3. Shinto believers
   a. 3,223,000 worldwide
   b. 3,220,000 in Asia
   c. 1,000 in North America
4. Adherents of Chinese folk religions including Taoists
   a. 187,107,000 worldwide
   b. 186,817,000 in Asia
   c. 122,000 in North America
5. Shamanists including followers of Bon
   a. 10,493,000 worldwide
   b. 10,233,000 in Asia
   c. 1,000 in North America

B. *Selected Literature*[18]
1. *Buddhist Temple of Chicago Bulletin.* Chicago: Buddhist Temple of Chicago (monthly).
2. *Crystal Mirror.* Berkeley, Calif.: Nyingma Tibetan Meditation Center (annual).
3. *Garunda.* Boulder, Colo.: Karma Dzong (annual).
4. *Gesar.* Berkeley, Calif.: Nyingma Tibetan Meditation Center (quarterly).
5. *International Buddhist Meditation Center Newsletter.* Los Angeles: International Buddhist Meditation Center (monthly).
6. *Journal of Chinese Religions,* Saskatoon, Canada: University of Saskatchewan (bulletin).
7. *The Journal of the Zen Mission Society.* Mt. Shasta, Calif.: Shasta Abbey (quarterly).
8. *Matava Buddhist Temple Newsletter.* Saginaw, Mich.: Matava Buddhist Temple.
9. *Mount Baldy Zen Center Newsletter.* Mount Baldy, Calif.: Mount Baldy Zen Center (quarterly).
10. *N.S.A. Quarterly.* Santa Monica, Calif.: Nichiren Shoshu Academy.
11. *Rinzai-ji Newsletter.* Los Angeles: Cimarron Zen Center (quarterly).

---

[18]This list includes a representative sample of Far Eastern religious journals and bulletins published in North America.

12. *Suchness.* Chicago: American Buddhist Association (quarterly).
13. *Tricycle: The Buddhist Review.* Denville, N.J.: Independent Buddhist magazine (quarterly).
14. *Vajra Bodhi Sea.* San Francisco: Sino-American Buddhist Association.
15. *Washington Buddhist.* Washington, D.C.: Washington Buddhist Vihara (bimonthly).
16. *Wheel of Dharma.* San Francisco: Buddhist Churches of America (monthly).
17. *Wind Bell.* San Francisco: Zen Center (quarterly).
18. *World Tribune.* Santa Monica, Calif.: Nichiren Shoshu of America (tri-weekly).
19. *ZCLA Journal.* Los Angeles: Zen Center of Los Angeles (quarterly).
20. *Zen Bow.* Rochester, N.Y.: Zen Center (quarterly).
21. *Zen Notes.* New York: First Zen Institute of American (monthly).

C. *Major Organizations*
1. Buddhist Churches of America (BCA)
   a. These churches belong to Jodo Shinshu (True Pure Land school).
   b. Nisaburo Hirano, a Japanese immigrant, established the first official Shinshu mission in San Francisco in 1899.
   c. Although the BCA is an independent organization, it contributes to the Hompa Hongwanji, the head temple of Jodo Shinshu, in Kyoto, Japan.
      (1) At one time the BCA was a mission of the Hompa Hongwanji.
      (2) Since the BCA is now autonomous, it receives no support from Japan.
   d. Most of its members are Japanese Americans with a small (though increasing) percentage of Caucasians, most who have joined because of marriage.
   e. Membership is estimated at over 50,000.
   f. "The BCA has served the Japanese-American community as a medium in which Japanese social and cultural values may be preserved and in which adaptation to the American culture may be expressed."[19]
2. Nichiren Shoshu of America
   a. The American branch of the Soka Gakkai is known as Nichiren Shoshu.[20]

---

[19]G. Baker, "Buddhism in America," in *The Perennial Dictionary of World Religions,* 137.

[20]Nichiren Buddhism comprises many sects in Japan; one is Nichiren Shoshu. The Soka Gakkai is a lay movement connected with the Nichiren Shoshu sect. The American branch of the Soka Gakkai is not known as Soka Gakkai but is known as Nichiren Shoshu because the parent organization is strongly tied in with Japanese nationalism and politics.

b. Masayasu Sadanaga started the organization with a few Japanese "war brides" after World War II.

c. Initially the members of Nichiren Shoshu in the United States were Japanese Americans, but in 1967 it began to attract Caucasians so that most members in North America are now Caucasians.

d. This organization's current membership is about 500,000 in North America.

3. Theravadins, Chinese Buddhists, Zen Buddhists, Tibetan Buddhists, and Taoists in North America are not devoted to a single organization but have numerous centers and monasteries throughout North America.

Part II: Theology

I. Human Suffering

A. *The Buddhist Position on Human Suffering Briefly Stated*[1]

1. All human life is grievous.
2. Ignorance and the desires of the senses lead to suffering.
3. Deliverance from suffering can be achieved through enlightenment.
4. Enlightenment is attained by obeying the Buddhist ethic.

B. *Arguments Used by Buddhists to Support Their Position on Human Suffering, Otherwise Known as the "Four Noble Truths"*

1. The First Noble Truth is *dukkha*.[2]

   a. Definition of *dukkha*

      (1) The general meaning of the word *dukkha* is "suffering," "pain," "misery," or "sorrow."

      (2) Buddhist scholars, however, regard this translation as highly unsatisfactory and misleading because it tends to give people the impression that Buddhist philosophy is pessimistic.

      (3) According to the Buddhist scholar Walpola Rahula, *dukkha* not only means "suffering," but it also comprises "deeper ideas such as 'imperfection,' 'impermanence,' 'emptiness,' 'insubstantiality.' It is difficult therefore to find one word to embrace the whole conception of the term *dukkha* as the First Noble Truth, and so it is better to leave it untranslated, than to give an inadequate and wrong idea of it by conveniently translating it as 'suffering' or 'pain.'"[3]

   b. The First Noble Truth's perspective on life

      (1) The Buddha's teaching on human suffering is neither optimistic nor pessimistic. Rather, it is realistic.

      (2) Buddhists view the Buddha as a spiritual physician. He neither ignores the problem and says all is well nor exaggerates the problem and gives up hope. Instead, he diagnoses the problem

---

[1]Whereas all religions have something to say about human suffering, this issue is central to all Buddhist philosophies. Taoism and the other Far Eastern religions will be excluded from this discussion because their participation is not necessary in understanding the difference between their belief systems and Christianity. In other words, the issue of suffering is not crucial to the other Far Eastern religions.

[2]*Dukkha* in Pali or *duhkha* in Sanskrit.

[3]Walpola Rahula, *What the Buddha Taught* (New York: Grove Press, 1974), 17.

objectively and correctly, "understands the cause and the nature of the illness, sees clearly that it can be cured, and courageously administers a course of treatment, thus saving his patient. . . . He is the wise and scientific doctor for the ills of the world."[4]

 c. The three aspects of *dukkha*

  (1) *Dukkha* is all forms of physical and mental suffering, which includes "birth, old age, sickness, death, association with unpleasant persons and conditions, separation from beloved ones and pleasant conditions, not getting what one desires, grief, lamentation, distress."[5]

  (2) *Dukkha* is change. Since all things are impermanent, pain, suffering, and unhappiness ultimately result. For example, a person is happy being with a loved one, but when that loved one is gone, that person becomes unhappy. Change has caused the suffering. The Buddha taught that there is happiness in life, but that inevitably that happiness will turn to sorrow.

  (3) *Dukkha* is the essence of life. Although people do not possess a soul, the energies that form a person are ever changing. Since life is impermanent and in constant flux, it is *dukkha*.

2. The Second Noble Truth is *samudaya*.

 a. The definition of *samudaya*

  (1) *Samudaya* means "arising of *dukkha*."

  (2) In other words, *samudaya* is the origin of suffering.

 b. The Second Noble Truth as *tanha*

  (1) *Tanha* means "craving" or "thirst."

  (2) Some Buddhist scholars refer to the Second Noble Truth as *tanha* because *tanha* leads to suffering.

  (3) *Tanha* is not the first or only cause of the arising of suffering, but it is the critical link in the causal chain that leads to suffering.

 c. The "Twelvefold Chain of Causation"

 The Buddha traced the cause of suffering to its origin as follows: "From ignorance as cause arise the aggregates [the energies or identity of a person], from the aggregates as cause arises consciousness, from consciousness as cause arises name-and-form (mind and body), from name-and-form as cause arises the sphere of the six (senses), from the sphere of the six as cause contact, from contact as cause sensation, from sensation as cause craving, from craving as cause grasping, from grasping as cause becoming, from

---

[4]Ibid.
[5]Ibid., 19.

becoming as cause birth, from birth as cause arise old age, death, grief, lamentation, pain, dejection, and despair. Even so is the origination of all this mass of pain."[6]

3. The Third Noble Truth is *nirodha*.
   a. The definition of *nirodha*
      (1) *Nirodha* means "cessation of *dukkha*."
      (2) In other words, *nirodha* reveals that there *is* liberation from suffering.
   b. *Nirodha* as nirvana
      (1) When one attains nirvana, one experiences *nirodha*.
      (2) For Buddhists, nirvana is not the extinction of self, since there is no self or soul to annihilate. Rather it is the annihilation of the illusion or false idea of self.[7]
      (3) In order to achieve nirvana, one must eliminate the main root of *dukkha* ("suffering"), which is *tanha* ("craving"). When craving is totally extinguished, *nirodha* occurs.
      (4) In addition, understanding the teachings of the Buddha not only removes ignorance, the primordial cause of suffering, but also paves the way for deliverance.

4. The Fourth Noble Truth is *magga*.
   a. The definition of *magga*
      (1) *Magga* means "the path leading to the cessation of *dukkha*."
      (2) *Magga* is also known as the "Middle Path," because it avoids the one extreme of seeking happiness through the senses and the other extreme of seeking truth through self-mortification.
   b. The Noble Eightfold Path
      (1) The Fourth Noble Truth comprises Buddhist ethics, which is known as the Noble Eightfold Path.
      (2) The Noble Eightfold Path is right understanding, right thought, right speech, right action, right livelihood, right effort, right mindfulness, and right concentration.
      (3) These eight categories of the Noble Eightfold Path are taught in order to perfect the three essentials of Buddhist training and discipline, namely, ethical conduct, mental discipline, and wisdom.
      (4) These eight categories of the Path are not stages that can be performed in succession or isolated from one another. Rather they are different dimensions of a total way of life.

---

[6]Edward J. Thomas, *The Life of Buddha as Legend and History* (London: Routledge & Kegan Paul, 1969), 193.
[7]Rahula, *What the Buddha Taught*, 37.

(5) The Buddha taught that suffering is the result of selfish desires or clinging and that they chain people to the wheel of insubstantial impermanent things. The Buddha's teachings aim at eliminating these selfish desires in ways described in the Fourth Noble Truth and at guiding the individual to nirvana or deliverance.

C. *Refutation of Arguments Used by Buddhists to Support Their Position on Suffering*[8]

1. The Buddhist teaching that human life is grievous is not in question.

   a. The Buddhist observation that people experience suffering of all sorts is an observable truth.

   b. In addition, the search for an explanation for human suffering is not only critical to Buddhism, but also to all philosophies and religions, including Christianity.

2. The Buddhist explanation for the cause and origin of suffering is incorrect.

   a. The implication of the Buddhist teaching on the cause of suffering

      (1) Buddhist doctrine asserts that the origin of one's suffering is ignorance and that the cause of that suffering is one's craving.

      (2) In essence, what Buddhist doctrine teaches is that we cause all the suffering we experience.

      (3) The following scenarios dispute that Buddhist doctrine.

   b. Victims of natural disasters

      (1) If a one-day-old baby is severely injured in an earthquake and then dies, is that baby responsible for its suffering?

      (2) The Buddhist will argue that what the baby did in its former life caused its present suffering.[9] Thus the baby is responsible for its suffering.

      (3) However, the cycle of life, death, and rebirth cannot be proven. Therefore, the Buddhist claim that one suffers because of what one has done in a previous life rests on an assumption that relies on no factual evidence.

   c. Victims of religious persecution

      (1) If a Christian is tortured in a society hostile toward Christianity because he or she refuses to reject Jesus Christ as God, is that Christian responsible for his or her suffering?

---

[8]Although many Buddhist scholars strongly insist that the term *suffering* is terribly inadequate in referring to the Buddhist concept of *dukkha*, I will still use it as an expression of this Buddhist concept since this term appears in most philosophical discussions on this topic.

[9]As a reminder, Buddhists teach that a person has no soul. Therefore, a soul is not reborn. The energy (aggregates) that form a person's identity is reborn.

      (2) The Buddhist will argue that the Christian is deluded into thinking that Jesus Christ is God. Such delusion causes suffering for the Christian.

      (3) The Buddhist explanation, however, rests on the belief that Christ is not God. Since the Buddhist cannot prove that Jesus Christ is not God, its argument is based solely on an unprovable assumption.

  d. Victims of crime

      (1) If a woman is savagely raped by a total stranger in her house, is she responsible for her suffering?

      (2) The Buddhist will argue that her suffering was due to the negative actions that she had previously done, though she had done nothing at the time to precipitate the assault.

      (3) The moral consciousness common to people throughout the world, however, would argue that she was an innocent victim of the crime, and every civilized judicial system would punish the guilty assailant, not the victim, of the crime.

      (4) Furthermore, if the woman's suffering was a result of a previous action on her part, then karma (cause and effect) forced her assailant to commit the crime. Therefore, his evil action was caused by her bad karma, for which he must then suffer.

      (5) In other words, the Buddhist in effect says that some people suffer grievously for a former act committed during a previous life while other people suffer for that which a higher force compelled them to do.

      (6) Victims of crime, however, are not responsible for what they suffered as a result of the crime, while criminals are responsible for committing their crimes.

3. The Buddhist assertion that there is deliverance from suffering can be accepted to a point.

  a. It is agreed that it is possible for human suffering to end (as will be shown in I.D.3 below).

  b. The Buddhist teaching that human suffering ceases through extinction is false.

      (1) Of course, if extinction of a person were possible, suffering would also cease.

      (2) Christ, however, taught that the wicked "will go away to eternal punishment, but the righteous to eternal life" (Matt. 25:46; see also 2 Thess. 1:9; Rev. 20:10–15).

      (3) In other words, people are immortal; they will not be extinguished.

4. The Buddhist quest for the cessation of suffering is misdirected.

  a. The Fourth Noble Truth of the Buddha is the Noble Eightfold Path.

(1) The purpose of the Noble Eightfold Path is to eliminate craving, which causes suffering.

(2) In effect, Buddhists ultimately seek escape from suffering.

b. The Bible disputes the Buddha's Fourth Noble Truth in two ways.

(1) The Bible does not teach that *all* desires are evil. In fact, we are to "desire" to do God's will (Ps. 40:8), "desire" God's mercy (Matt. 9:13), "desire" spiritual gifts (1 Cor. 12:31; 14:1), and "desire" to live honorably (Heb. 13:18).

(2) The Bible also teaches that the distinct purpose of Christ's coming to this world was to suffer on behalf of humanity's sins (Matt. 17:12; Mark 8:31; 9:12; Luke 24:26; Acts 3:18; 17:2–3; 26:22–23; Heb. 2:9–10, 18; 1 Peter 1:10–11; 2:21–24; 3:18; 4:1); that is, Christ purposely embraced suffering for us rather than attempting to avoid it.

c. The contrasting approaches to suffering by the Buddha and Christ is perhaps best described by Stephen Neill: "Why suffer? That is the ultimate question. It comes to sharp and challenging expression in the contrast between the serene and passionless Buddha and the tortured figure on the Cross. In Jesus we see One who looked at suffering with eyes as clear and calm as those of the Buddha. He saw no reason to reject it, to refuse it, to eliminate it. He took it into himself and felt the fullness of its bitterness and horror; by the grace of God he tasted death for every man. Others suffer; he will suffer with them and for them.... But he does not believe that suffering is wholly evil; by the power of God it can be transformed into a redemptive miracle. Suffering is not an obstacle to deliverance, it can become part of deliverance itself. And what he was he bids his children be—the world's sufferers, in order that through suffering the world may be brought back to God."[10]

D. Arguments Used to Prove the Biblical Doctrine on Suffering

1. The Bible regards human suffering as a crucial issue.

a. In fact, the Bible devotes an entire book to the issue of human suffering.

(1) In the book of Job, Job seeks to understand why he must suffer.

(2) God does not answer Job's specific question but helps him understand that he is sovereign and will ultimately bring about good for those who keep their trust in him.

b. The Bible indicates that all humans can expect to suffer and die (Job 5:7; 14:1, 10, 22).

---

[10]Stephen Neill, *Christian Faith and Other Religions* (London: Oxford University Press, 1970), 123.

    c. Nevertheless, the Bible makes a distinction between right and wrong kinds of suffering. Indeed, God commends those who suffer for doing good but not those who suffer for doing evil (1 Peter 2:19–20; 4:15).

    d. Therefore, even God's people should expect to suffer.

      (1) In fact, God's prophets during the Old Testament period suffered because they served the Lord (James 5:10).

      (2) The apostle Paul not only said that suffering is part of the Christian walk (Phil. 1:29) but also described his own hardships as a result of his Christian ministry (4:12).

      (3) The apostle Peter also taught that Christians should expect to suffer because of their faith in Christ (1 Peter 4:12).

      (4) Moreover, if we expect to share Christ's glory, we must also share his suffering (Rom. 8:17).

    e. Suffering for Christ serves a purpose.

      (1) When we suffer because of our faith in Christ, that suffering is one mark of God's favor upon us (1 Peter 4:14).

      (2) In addition, we can rejoice when we suffer in Christ because it strengthens our faith in God (James 1:2–4).

    f. Meanwhile, the blessings of God outweigh our sufferings.

      (1) For one thing, we receive God's overflowing comfort when we endure troubles (2 Cor. 1:3–5).

      (2) Most importantly, what we suffer is nothing compared to gaining Christ ourselves (Phil. 3:8).

  2. The Bible teaches that the origin of human suffering was when the first man and woman disobeyed God.

    a. The fall of Adam and Eve, the first man and woman

      (1) God had placed Adam and Eve in an earthly paradise and commanded them not to eat the fruit from the tree of the knowledge of good and evil (Gen. 2:17).

      (2) Both Adam and Eve disobeyed God's command by eating the forbidden fruit (Gen. 3:6).

      (3) God punished Adam and Eve by telling them how they and their descendants would suffer as a result of their sin (Gen. 3:16–19).

    b. The consequences of the Fall

      (1) Because of Adam's disobedience, all people are sinful by nature; and because all people are sinful by nature, they all must die (Rom. 5:12–14, 18–19).

      (2) Thus, all people die because of Adam (1 Cor. 15:22).

      (3) Eve also participated in the Fall (Gen. 3:6; 2 Cor. 11:3; 1 Tim. 2:14).

      (4) Because of their disobedience, all of creation is subject to suffering, decay, and death (Rom. 8:20–23).

  3. The Bible reveals that suffering will cease for those who finally enter God's heavenly kingdom.

    a. The present suffering of God's people is temporary.

      (1) God's people experience temporary suffering as those born again before entering into an imperishable inheritance (1 Peter 1:3–6).

      (2) That inheritance is the eternal glory Christians will have with the Lord in heaven, with which their earthly suffering cannot compare (2 Cor. 4:17–18).

      (3) In fact, God counts his people worthy to be in his heavenly kingdom because of what they have suffered for his sake (2 Thess. 1:4–5).

    b. God will end the suffering of his people.

      (1) Though God's people suffer because of their service to Christ, God will give the faithful ones the crown of life (Rev. 2:10).

      (2) God will wipe away every tear of his people in his heavenly kingdom, and there will be no more death, mourning, crying, or pain for them (Rev. 21:3–4).

  4. The Bible shows that Jesus' suffering and death atone for the sins of Christians, which guarantees that they won't have to suffer when they are finally united with Christ in heaven.

    a. Jesus atoned for the sins of God's people in order for them not to be punished for the wrongs they have done.

      (1) Although Christians experience chastisements and discipline in order to make them more Christlike, Jesus took the punishment for their sins upon himself so they won't have to suffer God's judgment for their transgressions unlike those who reject Christ (Isa. 53:5–6; 1 John 1:7; 2:2; 4:10).

      (2) Christ died once for all time for the sins of God's people in order to bring them to God (1 Peter 3:18).

      (3) Jesus suffered even unto death so he could perfect God's people, making them righteous before God (Phil. 3:9–11; Heb. 2:9–10).

    b. God's people will be united with Christ in heaven, where there is no suffering.

      (1) After God's people have suffered for a little while, God will call them to his eternal glory with Christ (1 Peter 5:10).

      (2) Because of God's love for his people, God has redeemed them in Christ so that when they get to heaven they will suffer no more (Rev. 21:3–4).

II. Human Soul

A. *The Buddhist Position on the Human Soul Briefly Stated*[11]

1. A being is composed of five aggregates.
2. Humanity has conceived the concept of a soul in its desire for self-preservation.
3. The false belief in a soul is the source for all of the evil in the world.

B. *Arguments Used by Buddhists to Support Their Position on the Human Soul*

1. The Buddhist doctrine of no-soul is known as *anatta*.[12]

   a. Buddhist teaching denies the existence of a permanent, unchanging entity that exists within a person. In other words, each person does not have a soul, self, or ego.

   b. Instead, human beings are comprised of the five aggregates.[13]

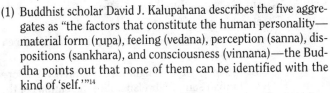

   (1) Buddhist scholar David J. Kalupahana describes the five aggregates as "the factors that constitute the human personality—material form (rupa), feeling (vedana), perception (sanna), dispositions (sankhara), and consciousness (vinnana)—the Buddha points out that none of them can be identified with the kind of 'self.'"[14]

   (2) The five aggregates are all impermanent, constantly changing, and temporarily connected.

   (3) Buddhists use the analogy of a chariot to describe the five aggregates.
   A human being is a collection of particular aggregates in the same way as a chariot is a collection of particular items. Just as the parts of a chariot can be taken apart and reformed to make something else, so also a human being dies and its aggregates reform to make another living being when it is reborn.

   c. Buddhists separate truths into conventional and ultimate truths.

   (1) Conventional truths allow for the expressions of "I," "me," and "individual" in daily discourse. Such expressions conforms to the conventions and languages of the world.

---

[11]Like the doctrine of suffering, the nature of the soul is not a major component in the belief systems of Taoism, Confucianism, Shinto, and Bon. Since ancestor worship is practiced in Confucianism and Shinto, an understanding that human beings have a spiritual dimension to their identity is present in these religions. Meanwhile, a cosmic life force inherent in human beings is presumed in Taoism and Bon. Nevertheless, since a systematic discussion of the human soul is absent in the fundamental doctrines of these religions, they will not be included in this section of the book.

[12]*Anatta* is the term in the Pali language; *anatman* is the same term in Sanskrit.

[13]These aggregates are known as *khandhas* or *skandhas* in Sanskrit.

[14]David J. Kalupahana, *Buddhist Philosophy: A Historical Analysis* (Honolulu: The University Press of Hawaii, 1976), 40.

35

        (2) Ultimate truths, however, comprehend the reality of no "I," "me," or "individual."

        (3) People can be designated in the conventional sense, but they have no being in reality.

    d. The Theravadins and Mahayanists define the doctrine of no-soul somewhat differently from each other.

        (1) Along with the doctrines of *dukkha* (suffering) and *anicca* (impermanence), *anatta* is a central tenet of Theravada Buddhism.

        (2) In contrast, "Mahayana Buddhism to some extent reestablished selfhood in its doctrines . . . as a kind of enduring subconscious, and of the Buddha nature as a kind of *true* selfhood found in every man. Yet even here there remains the sense of the empirical self's unreality."[15]

2. Buddhist doctrine rejects the belief in a soul.

    a. Human beings cling fanatically to the idea that they possess an eternal soul.

        (1) Ignorance, weakness, fear, and desire cause people to believe they have a soul.

        (2) Although other religions have a highly developed view of the human soul, their elaborate explanations of the human soul are nevertheless false mental projections based on false hopes.

        (3) Moreover, "these ideas are so deep-rooted in man, and so near and dear to him, that he does not wish to hear, nor does he want to understand, any teaching against them."[16]

    b. Unlike any other major spiritual teacher, the Buddha taught against the false belief in a human soul.

        (1) In fact, the Buddha's teachings on the soul conflict with the teachings of every other religion, especially with the Christian doctrine of the soul.

        (2) Only a very few people can comprehend the Buddhist truth that rejects the existence of a soul.

        (3) Individuals are enlightened when they finally destroy this desire for a soul.

        (4) The Buddha's teachings are neither negative nor annihilistic; it is simply reality, while it is "the false belief in a non-existing imaginary self that is negative."[17]

3. Buddhist doctrine teaches that *any* speculation about the human soul is harmful.

---

[15]H. C. Warren, "Anatta," in *The Perennial Dictionary of World Religions,* ed. Keith Crim (San Francisco: Harper & Row, 1989), 30.
[16]Rahula, *What the Buddha Taught,* 52.
[17]Ibid., 66.

    a. Insisting that a human soul exists generates further suffering individually and cosmically.

        (1) Clinging to the belief of a human soul produces harmful thoughts that cause selfish desires, hatred, conceit, pride, immorality, and delusion for the individual—all of which lead to personal suffering.

        (2) Furthermore, clinging to this belief "is the source of all the troubles in the world from personal conflicts to wars between nations. In short, to this false view can be traced all the evil in the world."[18]

    b. Buddhist teaching asserts that maintaining an opinion that no soul exists is also wrong.

        (1) Whether a person holds the view that he or she has a soul or does *not* have a soul is an obstacle to enlightenment. In other words, *all* philosophical speculation about the human soul obstructs people from attaining ultimate truth.

        (2) Instead, without engaging in the illusory tendencies of mental activity, the true spiritual seeker comprehends that "there is nothing permanent, everlasting, unchanging and eternal in the whole of existence."[19]

C. Refutation of Arguments Used by Buddhists to Support Their Position on the Human Soul

1. Buddhists claim that speculation about the human soul is harmful; however, they engage in the same kind of speculation while attempting to refute such speculation.

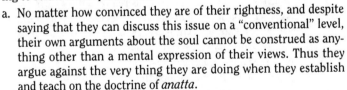

    a. No matter how convinced they are of their rightness, and despite saying that they can discuss this issue on a "conventional" level, their own arguments about the soul cannot be construed as anything other than a mental expression of their views. Thus they argue against the very thing they are doing when they establish and teach on the doctrine of *anatta*.

    b. Therefore, by their criticism of the Christian view of the soul, they must concede our right to express our views on the subject.

2. Buddhist statements against soul-affirming belief systems shatter the notion that Buddhism is a tolerant religion.

    a. Many Buddhists promote the idea in the West that Buddhism is tolerant of other religions and respectful of Christianity in particular.

        (1) Masaharu Anesaki, a former professor of Japanese studies at Harvard University, wrote, "There are many paths and roads in forests and valleys, but those who have climbed up to the hilltop

---

[18] Ibid., 51.
[19] Ibid., 66.

by any of these routes equally enjoy the same moonlight on the open summit."[20]

    (2) Anesaki quoted an old Buddhist proverb, articulating what many people in the West believe: Different religions may guide people along different paths but they all lead ultimately to the same goal or, in this case, summit.

  b. Devout Buddhists, however, know that this idea is not true. In fact, Buddhists not only teach that the Christian view of the human soul is fallacious but also that it causes evil and suffering in the world.

  c. Therefore, Christians need to express their views on the soul both to unmask the misconception that Buddhism is as tolerant as some claim it to be and to defend the Christian faith from false and scurrilous accusations. They especially need to point out that sin and suffering do not arise from a belief in or denial of the soul's existence, but from the soul itself.

3. The Buddhist contention that nirvana is blissful contradicts its teaching that no soul exists.

  a. The Buddhists believe that an enlightened being who realizes that there is no soul experiences perfect bliss.

    (1) Buddhists argue that nirvana is not annihilation of self, because there is no self to annihilate. Instead, it is craving that is annihilated. Therefore, they insist that Buddhist teaching on nirvana and no-soul is neither negative nor nihilistic as critics of Buddhism claim.

    (2) Accordingly, "he who has realized the Truth, Nirvana,[21] is the happiest being in the world," states Walpola Rahula. "He is joyful, exultant, enjoying the pure life, his faculties pleased, free from anxiety, serene and peaceful."[22]

  b. A human being, however, cannot be without a soul, self, or ego and still enjoy the sensations that accompany nirvana.

    (1) According to comparative religion scholar J. N. D. Anderson, "It is somewhat difficult, it is true, to see how a Buddhist who has reached a state [realization] of no-self (*an-atta*) can enjoy such bliss."[23]

---

[20]Masaharu Anesaki, "How Christianity Appeals to a Japanese Buddhist," *Hibbert Journal* 4, no. 1 (1905).

[21]Since the term *nirvana* has different meanings for different people, comprehending what a person may mean when they use this term can be quite difficult. In the context of Rahula's statement, nirvana is when one is enlightened to Ultimate Reality or Absolute Truth during one's lifetime. Meanwhile, *parinirvana* is the final passing away of the Buddhist saint after death. It is like the flame that is blown out. It is not a soul that is blown out, however, but that saint's aggregates. *Parinirvana* is frequently referred to as simply nirvana, thus the confusion.

[22]Rahula, *What the Buddha Taught*, 43.

[23]J. N. D. Anderson, *Christianity and Comparative Religion* (Downers Grove, Ill.: InterVarsity Press, 1970), 59.

(2) In short, it is unintelligible to claim that an enlightened being experiences the finest sensations of life, yet declaring that this enlightened being has no self with which to enjoy those sensations.

4. What Buddhists describe as not the soul is in many respects the soul according to Christian thinking.

   a. What is the soul?

   (1) Buddhists deny that each person possesses a separate soul that God has created and will judge as to whether it will eternally live in heaven or hell.[24] Buddhist disagreement with the Christian view of the origin, subsistence, and destiny of the human soul is unmistakable.[25]

   (2) Mere rejection of another religion's definition of a soul, however, does not preclude its own belief in the human soul.

   (3) In fact, what Buddhists believe is that human beings do possess *something* that is distinct from other individuals and that lives on after physical death. Whether they use the word "soul" to describe it is irrelevant. The issue here is not over the label but over the thing itself.

   b. The five aggregates are in some respects another way of describing particular operations of the human soul.

   (1) Buddhists assert that a human being has consciousness, matter, mental formations, perception, and sensations, but in no way can these aggregates be construed as attributes of the human soul.

   (2) While Christian theism rejects a materialistic conception of the soul, it does affirm that operations of the human soul include the mental functions listed above.[26]

   (3) In other words, if this *something* is aware of things like a soul, makes decisions like a soul, experiences sensations like a soul, and generally operates as a soul, no matter how strongly a Buddhist denies that it is a soul, it is a soul.

   c. In fact, many Buddhists believe and teach that they have something similar to a soul that goes to paradise or enjoys material and immaterial blessings in the present life.

   (1) For example, the Buddhist movement popular among the common people are the Amidist schools, which teach that

---

[24]Note that according to Christian teaching, all people will experience resurrection and thus will spend eternity with body and soul.

[25]Although modern Buddhist scholars have ardently argued against the Christian view of the human soul, it should be noted that the doctrine of *anatta* was conceived in reaction to the Hindu conception of the human soul (*atman*).

[26]Christian theologians classically have held to the soul's "simplicity," meaning that it is not composite or made up of discrete parts.

39

Buddhists who put their trust in Amida Buddha will go to the Western Paradise and be with their loved ones. What is that which will dwell and fellowship with other faithful Buddhists in paradise? It cannot be anything other than a soul.[27]

(2) Another example of this need to incorporate the human soul in their beliefs are members of Nichiren Buddhism. They chant for material and immaterial blessings. But why does this religion promise to reward true believers in this way if there is no soul which can enjoy these blessings?

(3) In other words, the doctrine of *anatta* (no-soul) is intolerable even for most Buddhists.

D. **Arguments Used to Prove the Biblical Doctrine of the Human Soul to Buddhists**

1. The ancient Hebrew conception of the human soul

a. The standard Hebrew word for "soul" in the Old Testament is *nephesh.*

(1) *Nephesh* refers to a "breathing" creature (Gen. 2:7). It describes an animated being.

(2) *Nephesh* may indicate the entire inner nature of a person (Ps. 31:9; 63:1).[28]

(3) *Nephesh* may also refer to a person's entire personality (Ps. 6:3; Isa. 26:9).

b. Most Bible scholars believe that the Hebrews did not generally view the human soul in opposition to the physical body.

(1) Although the Hebrews distinguished between body and soul, they did not elevate one above the other.

(2) The Hebrews also did not teach that humans are tripartite (body, soul, and spirit).

(3) According to Bible scholar George Eldon Ladd, the Hebrews' understanding of the human soul was that the "soul (*Nephesh*) is not a higher part of man standing over against his body but designates the vitality or life principle in man."[29]

c. The Hebrews did not refer to the human soul with technical discrimination. Instead, they had many designations for the inner person or the psychological aspects of personality.

---

[27]It should be said that though a faithful Buddhist may reside in paradise for a thousand years, a truly enlightened Buddhist will ultimately experience *parinirvana.*

[28]For a theological discussion of *nephesh*, see Bruce K. Waltke, "Nephesh," in the *Theological Wordbook of the Old Testament*, eds. R. Laird Harris, Gleason L. Archer, Jr., and Bruce K. Waltke (Chicago: Moody, 1980), 2:1395–98. See also Merrill F. Unger, "Soul," in *The New Unger's Bible Dictionary* (Chicago: Moody, 1988), 1213.

[29]George Eldon Ladd, *A Theology of the New Testament* (Grand Rapids: Eerdmans, 1974), 458. Note that the Hebrews thought of the soul (*nephesh*) not only as a life principle but also as the mind of a person. See Prov. 2:10 and 16:21–24, where references to the soul would otherwise mean the mind.

(1) It possess life (Gen. 2:7; Job 32:8; 33:4).

(2) It denotes the whole person (Lev. 17:11; Ps. 34:2; 103:1; Ezek. 18:4).

(3) It is the seat of human appetite (Job 33:20; Ps. 42:1).

(4) It is the source of emotion (Ps. 42:11; 62:5; 86:4: 94:19; Prov. 13:19; 16:24; Isa. 42:1; 55:2; Lam. 3:20).

(5) It is associated with the will (Deut. 6:5; 10:12; 30:6; Josh. 22:5; Ps. 24:4; 2 Kings 23:25).

2. The early Christian view of the human soul[30]

a. The standard Greek word for "soul" in the New Testament is *psuche.*

(1) Like *nephesh* in the Old Testament, *psuche* in the New Testament can mean the totality of a person (Luke 12:19; Acts 2:43; 3:23).

(2) However, along with "spirit," "heart," and other psychological terms, *psuche* normally stands for the immaterial makeup or aspect of humanity.

b. In fact, "soul" in the New Testament has various usages.

(1) "Soul" can simply mean "life" (Matt. 6:25; 16:26; 20:28; Luke 12:22; Acts 3:23; Rom. 16:4; 1 Cor. 15:45).

(2) "Soul" can apply to the moral aspects of a person (Heb. 13:17; James 1:21; 5:20; 1 Peter 1:9; 3 John 2). For example, "souls" responded to the Gospel (Acts 2:41; 14:22).

(3) "Soul" is also understood as being distinct from the body (Mark 8:35; Acts 2:27; Rev. 20:4). For example, Jesus made this distinction clear when he said, "Do not be afraid of those who kill the body but cannot kill the soul" (Matt. 10:28).

c. Furthermore, "key passages [in the New Testament] indicate a significant development upon the OT view of the soul."[31]

(1) Though entirely consistent with the Old Testament view, a shift in emphasis takes place from Old to New Testament thought.

(2) The Hebrews viewed *nephesh* more as a total spiritual being (a living conscious creature), whereas the New Testament writers generally presented the "soul" as one of the constituent elements in human psychology.

3. Modern Christian thought on the human soul

---

[30]For theological discussions on the early Christian view of the soul, see Geoffrey W. Bromiley, *Theological Dictionary of the New Testament,* abridged in one volume (Grand Rapids: Eerdmans, 1985), 1342–53; and D. M. Lake, "Soul," in *The Zondervan Pictorial Encyclopedia of the Bible* (Grand Rapids: Zondervan, 1976), 5:496–98.

[31]D. M. Lake, "Soul," 5:497.

a. Although the Christian church has not universally accepted a single metaphysical definition of the human soul, Baptist theologian Augustus Strong's statements on the human soul typify the views of most conservative Christians.

   (1) "Man has a two-fold nature," he said, "on the one hand material, on the other hand immaterial. He consists of body, and of spirit, or soul."[32]

   (2) Strong further elaborated on the dichotomous theory, stating, "the immaterial part of man, viewed as an individual and conscious life, capable of possessing and animating a physical organism, is called [*psuche*]; viewed as a rational and moral agent, susceptible of divine influence and indwelling, this same immaterial part is called [*pneuma*]."[33]

   (3) Theologians Louis Berkhof and Charles Hodge also adopt this view of the human soul.[34]

b. Therefore, a significant distinction exists between the Buddhist doctrine of *anatta* and the Christian concept of the human soul.

   (1) The devout Buddhist believes that as a truly enlightened being he or she will ultimately be extinguished like the candle flame.

   (2) Meanwhile, the faithful Christian believes as a sanctified disciple of Jesus Christ she or he will one day enter the eternal heavenly light of the Savior and enjoy intimate fellowship with God forever (Rev. 6:9; 20:4).

III. The Doctrine of "Emptiness"

A. The Buddhist Position on "Emptiness" Briefly Stated[35]

1. All that exists is relative and nonsubstantial.
2. All that exists is empty of lasting value.
3. True recognition of the emptiness of all things totally frees a person from the attachment to all things and ultimately delivers that person from suffering.

B. Arguments Used by Buddhists to Support Their Position on "Emptiness"

1. The Buddhist doctrine of *shunyata*[36]

---

[32]Augustus Strong, *Systematic Theology* (Westwood, N.J.: Revell, 1907), 483.
[33]Ibid., 486.
[34]Louis Berkhof, *Systematic Theology* (Grand Rapids: Eerdmans, 1939), 194–95; and Charles Hodge, *Systematic Theology*, 3 vols. (Grand Rapids: Eerdmans, 1952), 2:42–51.
[35]The Buddhist doctrine of "emptiness" is unique to the Buddhist religion, and it was developed into a sophisticated philosophical system in Mahayana Buddhism, particularly the Madhyamika and Yogacara schools. In addition, the doctrine of emptiness should be studied to understand Zen Buddhism.
[36]*Shunyata* or *ʻsunyata* is the term for "emptiness" in the Sanskrit language; *ʻsunya* or *ʻsunyam* is the term for "empty" in Sanskrit.

a. *Shunyata* literally means "suchness," "openness," "voidness," or simply "absolute nothingness."

b. *Shunyata,* however, is most commonly known as "emptiness."

2. The Buddhist doctrine of *anicca*[37]

a. *Anicca* literally means "not enduring." It asserts the doctrine of impermanence, that is, nothing is permanent.

b. Along with "suffering" (*dukkha*) and "no-soul" (*anatta*), "impermanence" (*anicca*) is the third pillar of the Buddhist philosophy. Comprehending the doctrine of impermanence is key to understanding the doctrine of emptiness.

c. Since all things are temporary, they are constantly changing and always in flux. In other words, they are relative and nonsubstantial.

d. Therefore, all things are empty of self-reality.

3. No lasting value for all phenomena

a. People should not be attached to anything, including their ideas and perceptions of themselves, because nothing is permanent. Otherwise they will be bound to the misery of perpetual rebirths.

b. Furthermore, any notion or act is empty of inherent good or bad.

4. Total freedom through understanding the emptiness of all things

a. "To become aware of the impermanence of all that exists in time and space, including oneself, is a step toward enlightenment."[38]

b. In fact, when one has such understanding, one is free to truly experience the richness of life as a serene, compassionate being, as the Buddha was.

C. *Refutation of Arguments Used by Buddhists to Support Their Position on "Emptiness"*

1. The conflict between the doctrines of *anicca* and *dukkha*

a. Buddhist philosophy asserts that all things are impermanent.

b. Also according to Buddhist philosophy, unless a person is enlightened to the emptiness of all things, the suffering of that person is absolute.

c. Both beliefs demonstrate an inherent contradiction in what Buddhists teach concerning the essence (*anicca*) of a person and the condition (*dukkha*) of a person.

d. For example, Buddhist philosophy implies that a Christian who refuses to recant his or her belief in Christ is doomed to permanent suffering, and yet according to Buddhist philosophy the suffering of the Christian is impermanent.

---

[37]While *anicca* is a term from the Pali language, *anitya* is the same term from Sanskrit.
[38]W. L. King, "Anicca," in *The Perennial Dictionary of World Religions,* 37.

e. Although contradictions within the Buddhist philosophical system do not alarm Buddhists because they regard such contradictions as false perceptions of intellectual delusion, their assertions violate common sense.

2. The conflict between the Noble Eightfold Path and *shunyata*

  a. Buddhism is a highly ethical religion.

    (1) The Fourth Noble Truth of the Buddha contains the Buddhist ethics, which include right views, right speech, right conduct, and so on (see I.B.4.b. above in "Part II: Theology").

    (2) According to the Buddha, these ethics guide a person along the path to enlightenment.

  b. Nevertheless, Buddhists also teach that all things are empty of value.

    (1) In short, there is no rightness or wrongness, since rightness and wrongness are, among other things, statements of value.

    (2) In fact, Masao Abe, a leading interpreter of Zen to the West, acknowledges that Christians may understandably raise the question, "If judgment, including the distinction between good and evil, is completely reciprocal or reversible [speaking of *shunyata*], how can human ethics be established?"[39]

    (3) Abe offers a Buddhist answer to this criticism of the doctrine of emptiness by saying, "Shunyata is fundamentally Non-Shunyata. . . . This means that true Shunyata empties itself as well as everything else. Through its self-emptying it makes everything exist as it is and work as it does."[40]

    (4) In effect, this answer affirms the contradiction by saying that the contradiction is unimportant in light of a greater truth, which is incomprehensible to a non-Buddhist.

    (5) Their affirmation of contradictions, however, thereby allows for their statement "Buddhism is true and Christianity is false" to be taken to mean "Buddhism is false and Christianity is true." Thus the Buddhist cannot argue effectively that Christian teachings are wrong while affirming inherent contradictions within their own doctrines.

  c. The ultimate result of this conflict between Buddhist ethics and *shunyata* is the diminution of an absolute, personal God.

    (1) Despite the Buddhist quest to live a moral life, the Buddhist must ultimately admit that no eternal, sovereign God exists

---

[39]See Masao Abe, "Kenosis and Emptiness," in *Buddhist Emptiness and Christian Trinity,* eds. Roger Corless and Paul F. Knitter (New York: Paulist, 1990), 21.
[40]Ibid., 22.

who has established an ethical standard by which humans should live.

(2) Although "love becomes the overarching principle of ethical and moral conduct for the Buddhist," says George A. Mather and Larry A. Nichols, "Missing . . . is an ethic of love directed to God."[41]

3. The conflict between the Twelvefold Chain of Causation and *parinirvana*

a. The Buddhist doctrine of causation

(1) According to the Buddha, human experience is cyclical and causal, which he systematized in a twelvefold formula, known as the Twelvefold Chain of Causation.[42]

(2) Ignorance gives rise to, or causes, aggregates, which gives rise to consciousness, and so on to suffering, and then the cycle continues all over again.

(3) Unless one is enlightened, he or she is bound to this chain of causation.

(4) Furthermore, "in Buddhism," states David J. Kalupahana, "the causal pattern is recognized even in the psychic, moral, social, and spiritual realms."[43]

(5) In short, cause and effect governs all of life.

b. The unexplainable paradox

(1) Buddhist philosophy, however, also asserts that people are impermanent and that all aspects of who they are constantly in flux.

(2) And yet Buddhists teach that it is possible for people to achieve enlightenment and then *parinirvana,* or extinction.

(3) Now, how is it possible for impermanent beings within the chain of cause and effect to have the power within themselves to break the chain of causation?

(4) Moreover, Buddhism rules out any higher being breaking the chain for a human being. "Man's position, according to Buddhism, is supreme," declares Walpola Rahula. "Man is his own master, and there is no higher being or power that sits in judgment over his destiny."[44]

(5) Left to himself or herself, it is inconceivable that any impermanent being can attain deliverance from the chain of suffer-

---

[41]George A. Mather and Larry A. Nichols, *Dictionary of Cults, Sects, Religions, and the Occult* (Grand Rapids: Zondervan, 1993), 47–48.

[42]See Part II, I.B.2.c.

[43]Kalupahana, *Buddhist Philosophy,* 27.

[44]Rahula, *What the Buddha Taught,* 1.

ing. But Rahula has an answer for this criticism: "Nirvana is beyond logic and reasoning."[45]

(6) On that we can say, "Yes, it is."

D. Arguments Used to Prove the Biblical Doctrine of Permanent, Unchanging Things to Buddhists

1. The Christian view of eternity

    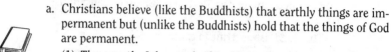

    a. Christians believe (like the Buddhists) that earthly things are impermanent but (unlike the Buddhists) hold that the things of God are permanent.

    (1) The apostle John made this distinction clear when he said, "The world and its desires pass away, but the man who does the will of God lives forever" (1 John 2:17). Note that Scripture says the desire for worldly things will pass away, but *we* will not.

    (2) Furthermore, the apostle Paul taught that "Our light and momentary troubles are achieving for us an eternal glory that far outweighs them all" (2 Cor. 4:17). Note that *suffering* will also pass away, but that the glory God gives us will not.

    (3) Paul then added, "So we fix our eyes not on what is seen, but on what is unseen. For what is seen is temporary, but what is unseen is eternal" (2 Cor. 4:18).

    b. Scripture teaches that the triune God is eternal.

    (1) God himself is eternal (Deut. 33:27).

    (2) Jesus Christ, his Son, is eternal (Rev. 1:18).

    (3) The Holy Spirit is eternal (Heb. 9:14).

    c. Furthermore, the things of God are eternal.

    (1) His power is eternal (Rom. 1:20).

    (2) His purposes are eternal (Eph. 3:11).

    (3) His judgments are eternal (Heb. 6:2).

    (4) The redemption he performed is eternal (Heb. 9:12).

    (5) The salvation he gives is eternal (Heb. 5:9).

    d. The soul of every person is eternal.

    (1) Those people who are in Christ have eternal life with God in heaven (Matt. 25:46; Mark 10:29–30; John 3:15; 6:54; 10:28; 17:2; Rom. 2:7; 6:23; 1 Tim. 1:16; Titus 1:2; 1 John 2:25; 5:11, 13, Jude 21).

    (2) Even the lost will live forever, but in damnation (Matt. 25:46; Jude 7).

    e. Most importantly, the character of God and of Jesus Christ is permanent and never changing (Mal. 3:6). Indeed, "Jesus Christ is the same yesterday and today and forever" (Heb. 13:8).

---

[45]Ibid., 43.

2. The Christian view of good and evil
   a. Christianity affirms the existence of good and evil.
      (1) Scripture says that God is good (Ps. 34:8; 86:5; 100:5; 2 Chron. 7:3; 1 Peter 2:3).
         (a) In fact, God is so good that he cannot look upon evil with favor (Hab. 1:13).
         (b) In addition, what God does is good (Ps. 119:68).
         (c) And, of course, Jesus Christ, his Son, is good (John 10:11).
      (2) Meanwhile, Scripture often speaks of the evil one (Matt. 6:13; John 17:15; Eph. 6:16; 2 Thess. 3:3; 1 John 2:13–14; 5:18–19).
         (a) In fact, the evil one is the devil (1 John 3:10, 12).
         (b) In addition, Paul warned Christian believers that they are at war with the spiritual forces of evil in the heavenly realms (Eph. 6:12).
   b. Scripture also teaches that God has established a standard of right and wrong for people to observe.
      (1) God commanded Adam, the first man, not to eat the fruit of the tree of the knowledge of good and evil (Gen. 2:9, 17), thus providing a standard of right and wrong behavior, which is obeying or disobeying God.
      (2) Throughout Scripture, people are told to "turn from evil and do good" (Ps. 34:14).
      (3) Doing good means obeying God's laws, which themselves are good (Rom. 7:12, 16).
      (4) The Gospel, which is God's news about salvation in Christ Jesus, is also called "good" (Mark 16:15).
      (5) In addition, mature Christians can distinguish good from evil (Heb. 5:14).
   c. Finally, God will judge whether people will go to heaven or hell.
      (1) God will judge every person's action, whether it is good or evil (Eccl. 12:14).
      (2) Yet, Scripture also teaches that no one is righteous and does good (Rom. 3:10, 12).
      (3) God, however, has made righteous those who are in Christ (Rom. 5:17–19).
      (4) After the Lord judges the righteous and the wicked, he will receive the righteous to be with him forever in heaven and send the wicked to eternal punishment in hell (Matt. 25:31–33, 46).
3. The Christian view of causation
   a. Humanity is enslaved to sin.
      (1) Sin entered the world when the first man and woman disobeyed God (see Gen. 3:1–19).

(2) Every person has inherited a sinful nature because the first man sinned (Rom. 5:12, 19; Eph. 2:3).

(3) Since each person is sinful by nature, none of them does good (Ps. 14:1–3; 53:1–3; Eccl. 7:20; Rom. 3:10–12).

(4) The one exception is Jesus Christ, who was tempted in every way and yet was without sin (Heb. 4:15; 1 Peter 2:22; 1 John 3:5).

(5) Thus every other person is enslaved to the bondage of sin (John 8:34; Rom. 6:16–23).

b. Freedom from sin does not come from self-enlightenment, but through the atoning work of Jesus Christ.

(1) Jesus delivered us from sin by dying for our sins on the cross (Rev. 1:5).

(2) Thus Christ has set his followers free (John 8:36; Gal. 5:1) from the law of sin and death (Rom. 8:2), that is, from the causal effects of sin. And ultimately he has freed us from suffering as well (Rev. 21:4).

(3) Furthermore, Christians enjoy freedom by being in the Holy Spirit (2 Cor. 3:17).

(4) What God has done for us through Jesus Christ demonstrates how highly he values us. Indeed, Jesus said to his followers, "Consider the ravens: They do not sow or reap, they have no storeroom or barn; yet God feeds them. And how much more valuable you are than birds!" (Luke 12:24).

(5) How can we be "nothing" (*sunyata*), when God has such great love for us?

IV. The Doctrines of Salvation[46]

A. *Major Far Eastern Positions on Salvation[47] Briefly Stated*

1. Theravada Buddhism—One must renounce the world, become a monk, and deny one's selfish desires in order to attain salvation.

2. Zen Buddhism—One must be disciplined in the practice of meditation in order to effect salvation.

3. Amida Buddhism—One must put his or her faith in the almighty compassion of Amida Buddha in order to receive salvation.

---

[46]This section will include only the doctrines of those religions that have major impact on religious life in North America. Therefore, the teachings of Theravada Buddhism, Zen Buddhism, Amida Buddhism, Nichiren Buddhism, Tibetan Buddhism, Taoism, and Confucianism will be discussed under the subject of salvation.

[47]Of course, the term *salvation* is used very loosely here since what is meant can be quite different from one religion to another.

4. Nichiren Buddhism—One must chant an incantation from the Lotus Sutra in order to achieve salvation.

5. Tibetan Buddhism—One must engage in esoteric spiritual techniques in order to reach salvation more quickly.

6. Taoism—One must seek harmony with the world through passivity in order to realize salvation.

7. Confucianism—One must live by the ethical conduct taught by Confucius in order to experience salvation.

B. *Arguments Used by Far Eastern Religions to Support Their Positions on Salvation*

1. Theravada Buddhism

   a. A monastic Buddhist in Theravada Buddhism is called an "arhant."[48]

   (1) An arhant is one who has attained the highest stage of perfection in Theravada Buddhism.

   (2) An arhant is a person who has reached the end of the Eightfold Path of the Buddha's Fourth Noble Truth; that is, an arhant is "one who is free from all fetters, defilements and impurities through the realization of Nirvana in the fourth and final stage, and who is free from rebirth."[49]

   (3) In addition, arhants are free from the causal effects of karma because they have freed themselves from the false idea of self and from "clinging."

   (4) When an arhant dies, he or she is fully extinguished like a flame gone out. Salvation for an arhant is attaining *parinirvana*, the liberation from the cycle of rebirth (i.e., ceasing to exist).

   (5) To the Theravadins, Gautama the Buddha is the most famous among all arhants. He led the way for other arhants to follow.

   b. How arhants achieve salvation

   (1) Arhants must renounce the world and all its attachments, enter a Buddhist monastic order as a monk or nun, and detach themselves from all desires.

   (2) The requirement to being born an arhant is that the arhant has gone through specific stages of spiritual discipline in previous lives, each life breaking further away from the wheel of becoming (the cycle of rebirth). In short, one's effort to achieve salvation requires many lives dedicated to the teachings of the Buddha.

[48]*Arhant* in Pali literally means "worthy one." Sanskrit variants include *arhat, arhan,* and *arahant.* This Indian term predated the Buddha, but Buddhists took it and applied a more specific meaning to it.

[49]Rahula, *What the Buddha Taught,* 142.

(3) Furthermore, salvation can be achieved only by the arhant without any external help.

2. Zen Buddhism

a. Zen Buddhists seek salvation by experiencing *satori,* which is the Japanese term for enlightenment.

(1) Satori is the sudden awakening to one's true nature.

(2) When Zen Buddhists realize their Buddha nature, they experience inner joy and peace.

(3) Through the continued practice of meditation, Zen Buddhists can experience satori many times, each bringing them into deepening levels of self-awareness.

(4) Like all Buddhists, the ultimate goal of a Zen Buddhist is to reach *parinirvana* (extinction), but unlike other Buddhists, the immediate goal of the Zen Buddhist is to experience satori.

b. How Zen Buddhists experience satori

(1) *Zazen* (seated meditation) and *sanzen* (interviews with a Zen master) are spiritual techniques used to achieve satori.

(2) During meditation, Zen Buddhists use *koans* (irrational phrases) to cut through rational thinking and discriminating thought to attain non-thinking. "Non-thinking," said the thirteenth-century Japanese Zen patriarch Dogen, "that is the essential art of Zazen."[50]

(3) Satori can be attained only through self-effort (*jiriki*). Zen masters can help, but "you yourself must make the effort" says the *Dhammapada*. "Buddhas do but point the way."[51]

3. Amida Buddhism

a. Buddhists of the Pure Land schools believe they are saved because of the compassion of Amida Buddha.

(1) According to Buddhist tradition, millions of years ago a monk by the name of Dharmakara decided to become a bodhisattva[52] and purify a land known as the Western Paradise (Pure Land).

(2) The Amida Buddha (or Amitabha) now resides in *Sukhavati* (Pure Land).

(3) Because Amida Buddha accumulated innumerable merits due to his countless good deeds, faithful followers of Amida Buddha are reborn in this Western Paradise.

---

[50]From *Fukan Zazengi.*

[51]The *Dhammapada* is a book of the Buddhist canon, which contains verses covering Buddhist teaching. An anonymous Buddhist collected these verses, which are believed to have been the original teachings of the Buddha.

[52]Bodhisattvas are enlightened beings who postpone *parinirvana* to aid other human beings in their quest for enlightenment.

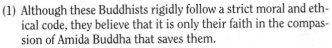

(4) These followers are devout Buddhists in the Jodoshu (School of the Pure Land) and Jodo Shinshu (True School of the Pure Land) Buddhism.

(5) Gods and men dwell in *Sukhavati,* but not animal or evil spirits. It is also free from all pain and suffering.

(6) Although an Amida Buddhist can remain in this Western Paradise for thousands of years, it is still a temporary abode before the Buddhist attains *parinirvana* (extinction).

b. Faithful devotion to Amida Buddha is what saves Buddhists in the Pure Land schools.

(1) Although these Buddhists rigidly follow a strict moral and ethical code, they believe that it is only their faith in the compassion of Amida Buddha that saves them.

(2) Thus, in Amida Buddhism, salvation is through the reliance on an outside source (*tariki*), and not self-effort (*jiriki*).

(3) They also believe that calling on the name of Amida Buddha, the simple repetition of *Namu Amida Butsu* (or *Nembutsu*), assures Buddhist believers of their salvation.

(4) "The nembutsu," says Buddhist scholar E. Dale Saunders, "was to be recited (1) with a sincere heart, that is, with genuine devotion, (2) with a deeply believing heart, and (3) with a longing heart, that is, with a desire, implemented by the merits of preceding existences, to attain birth in Amida's Pure Land."[53]

4. Nichiren Shoshu Buddhism

a. Nichiren Buddhists believe that chanting the invocation *Namu myo-ho-renge-kyo* ("Hail to the Wonderful Truth of the Lotus Sutra") saves them.

(1) According to Nichiren Buddhists, the Buddha gave the Lotus Sutra to supercede all of his other teachings because the Lotus Sutra is the essence of his doctrine.

(2) The invocation *Namu myo-ho-renge-kyo* embodies the mystical essence of the Lotus Sutra.

(3) Nichiren Buddhists believe that they will be in harmony with the laws of the universe and the fundamental flow of life by maintaining a rigorous and daily discipline of chanting this invocation.

(4) In addition, chanting this invocation is said to empower them with personal control over their lives, bringing them material and spiritual benefits, thus giving them true happiness.

(5) "The true intention of [Nichiren Shoshu Buddhism]," says Nichiren Buddhist scholar and leader Daisaku Ikeda, "is to save

[53]E. Dale Saunders, *Buddhism in Japan* (Philadelphia: University of Pennsylvania Press, 1971), 195.

the whole world through the attainment of each individual's happiness in life."[54]

(6) In short, while Nichiren Buddhists say they ultimately seek to experience *parinirvana,* their immediate goal is personal happiness.

b. The Nichiren Buddhists worship the *Gohonzon* and chant the *Daimoku* in order to achieve salvation.

(1) Nichiren Buddhists daily kneel before the Gohonzon, an altar that is the central object of their worship.

(2) The Gohonzon houses a mandala,[55] which has inscribed the sacred names of Nichiren and another Buddha mentioned in the Lotus Sutra and the Daimoku: *Namu myo-ho-renge-kyo.*

(3) Before the Gohonzon, the Nichiren Buddhists recite passages from the Lotus Sutra and chant the Daimoku. Nichiren claimed that repeatedly praying *Namu myo-ho-renge-kyo* is sufficient to bring enlightenment, or salvation, to his followers.

5. Tibetan Buddhism

a. Tibetan Buddhists employ tantras in their religious practices in order to attain salvation more quickly than other Buddhists.

(1) Tantrism is a mystical belief system that incorporates magical procedures in the attainment of occult powers. This system was articulated in esoteric documents known as *tantras* in the sixth century A.D. in India. Tantric Buddhists use tantras in their quest for enlightenment.

(2) The total dedication to the quest for enlightenment through the use of tantras is known as the Short Path. The Short Path employs spiritual techniques to reach enlightenment much more quickly through far fewer lifespans than would otherwise be accomplished through other Buddhist practices.

(3) Since spiritual aids in tantrism are extremely powerful and dangerous according to Tantric Buddhists, they urge that tantras be used only under the instruction and supervision of a trained Tantric Buddhist master.

(4) Thus the Eightfold Path of the Buddha is secondary to the Short Path of tantrism. "Devotees entering upon the Short Path," says John Blofeld, "are taught that henceforth they must do more than practice virtue and eschew evil."[56]

[54]Daisaku Ikeda, "Soka Gakkai," in *Lectures on Buddhism* (Tokyo: Seikyo Press, 1969), 4:15.

[55]A Buddhist mandala typically is designed with the Buddha in the center and other subordinate deities located in geometric proportion from the Buddha according to their importance in the Mahayana pantheon of that particular Buddhist religion. The Buddhist mandala presents a spiritual blueprint of the universe. Buddhists meditate on the mandala in order to mystically heighten their spiritual experience, bringing them to a fuller awareness of their Buddha nature.

[56]John Blofeld, *The Tantric Mysticism of Tibet* (New York: E. P. Dutton, 1970), 88.

(5) Tantrism is most visible in North America in the form of Tibetan Buddhism. "The Tantric tradition in America," says Emma Layman, "is expressed in three modes of practice—that of Tibetan and Mongolian Buddhism (sometimes called 'Lamaism'), the practice of the Japanese Shingon sect, and the mountain practice of the Shugendo of Japan. Of these, the tantrism of Tibet is the only one which has had any substantial impact in America."[57]

b. The Tibetan Buddhists utilize mantras, yantras, mudras, and other occultic techniques to reach their spiritual goals.

(1) Tibetan Buddhists believe that mantras are mystic syllables that will empower their meditations so that they can penetrate the Absolute and communicate with divine spirits. Their most sacred mantra is *Om Mani Padme Hum.*

(2) The yantra is the visual technique of Eastern meditation. The Buddhist meditates on a visual representation of the cosmos. The Buddhist mandala is a yantra that reveals to the meditator secret forces that emanate from within his or her own consciousness.

(3) The mudras are bodily gestures that accompany meditation. Hand gestures are particularly significant in contacting Buddhist deities.

(4) In addition to these spiritual techniques is the prayer wheel (*manicho-khor*) in Tibetan Buddhism. Tibetan Buddhists enlist their prayer wheels to propel them to enlightenment.

(a) A prayer wheel is a cylinder that has a sacred phrase written on it and contains a scroll with other sacred phrases.

(b) Tibetan Buddhists rotate the prayer wheel clockwise in order to actualize the forces related to the phrases.

(5) Thus Tibetan Buddhists emphasize sacramental action, rather than faith or wisdom. "The human body," says K. K. S. Chen, "is not deprecated but is valued as the instrument through which actions are performed to achieve salvation."[58]

6. Taoism

a. Taoists find salvation in the *Tao.*

(1) Taoists seek to reconcile *yin* and *yang,* the dual qualities of all life and creation. Yin and yang are principles of change: Yin is the female, passive principle; yang is the male, active principle. When they are in right balance, the Taoists achieve harmony with the Tao ("the Way").

---

[57]Emma McCloy Layman, *Buddhism in America* (Chicago: Nelson-Hall, 1976), 82.
[58]K. K. S. Chen, "Buddhism," in *The Perennial Dictionary of World Religions,* 133.

53

(2) "Tao," says D. C. Yu, "cannot be known through the conventional use of words. The only way to understand the Tao is through intuition, the attitude that does not discriminate or make distinctions about things but responds immediately or spontaneously."[59]

(3) Thus, perceiving reality in dualistic terms hinders one's comprehension of the Tao. Good and evil, right and wrong, true and false, and other dualities are relative perceptions. "'Right' and 'wrong' are just words which we may apply to the same thing," says Herrlee Creel, "depending upon which partial viewpoint we see it from. For each individual there is a different 'true' and a different 'false.' From the transcendent standpoint of the tao all such things are irrelevant."[60]

(4) In short, the Taoist holds that one should not make moral judgments or act in a discriminating way. Otherwise he or she will clash with nature and bring disharmony into his or her life.

(5) "It might further be argued," says James R. King, "that the Tao brings salvation in the sense that it makes possible freedom from distress or perturbation, opening the way to harmony between nature and the world of man."[61]

b. Taoists seek salvation in two distinct ways.

(1) Religious Taoists use magical, cultic, and esoteric techniques in their quest for immortality and spiritual power. Shamans and the occult are major features of their rituals.

(2) Philosophical Taoists believe that nonaction and passivity are necessary in order to be at one with the Tao. They hold that contemplative stillness (i.e., avoiding any physical and mental activity contrary to the forces and principles of nature) is how one can be in harmony with nature.

7. Confucianism

a. Confucianists seek to cultivate moral relationships and social harmony.

(1) Confucius taught an ethical doctrine that had its roots in the ancient traditions of China and that included his own thoughts on moral conduct of the individual in society.

(2) Confucius believed that the human condition could be socially determined and that universal happiness could be attained through social reform and justice.

---

[59]D. C. Yu, "Taoism, Philosophical," in *The Perennial Dictionary of World Religions*, 739.

[60]Herrlee Creel, *What Is Taoism and Other Studies in Chinese Culture* (Chicago: University of Chicago Press, 1970), 3.

[61]C. George Fry, James R. King, Eugene R. Swanger, and Herbert C. Wolf, *Great Asian Religions* (Grand Rapids: Baker, 1984), 115. Although a Christian publisher printed this book, it was a historical rather than a polemical presentation.

(3) Confucius indicated that people have both good and evil tendencies. Subsequently, Confucianism diverged into two major traditions along those lines.

(a) Mencius, who founded the idealist tradition, stressed the natural goodness of people, citing the importance of education and training in the nurture of character. Thus personal moral cultivation leads to a harmonious society.

(b) Hsun Tzu, who established the realist tradition, contended that human nature has uncivilized impulses that must be restrained and retrained by a strong society. Thus government is responsible for elevating the moral character of its people.

(4) In either case, Confucianism views the individual and society as interdependent in achieving peace and order in the world.

b. Salvation for the Confucianists is living a life according to the ethics of Confucius.

(1) The ethical code of Confucius is portrayed in his description of the ideal man[62] known as *chun-tzu* (lit. "son of a ruler"). Prior to Confucius, this term signified a member of the aristocracy. Confucius, however, transformed this term to designate the character of a person rather than his birth.

(2) *Chun-tzu* became the term for the "ideal gentleman" in Confucianism. *Chun-tzu* was a "man who never lost sight of virtue regardless of hardships endured and who always found fault with his own shortcomings rather than blaming others."[63]

(3) This ideal man displays the Five Constant Virtues, which are "gravity, generosity of soul, sincerity, earnestness, and kindness."[64] These virtues collectively produce "humaneness" (*jen*) in one's character.

(4) To attain "humaneness" the Confucianist practices "reciprocity" (*shu*), which can be summed up in Confucius's famous aphorism: "What you do not want done to yourself, do not do to others."[65]

(5) Since Confucius did not speculate about spiritual matters, following his teachings is more a philosophy of living than a practicing of religion. Thus salvation is more a matter of being at

---

[62]Women play a minor role in Confucius's teachings on ethical conduct and moral relationships. For example, he taught extensively about the relationship between a father and a son, but said little about motherhood. This is why his teachings focus on "the ideal man."

[63]R. L. Taylor, "Confucius," in *The Perennial Dictionary of World Religions*, 192.

[64]*Analects* 17:6. The *Analects* is a treatise by Confucius, composed of his sayings. It is one of the Four Books. The Confucian canon consists of the Five Classics and the Four Books.

[65]*Analects* 15:23.

peace with one's self and the world than attaining some spiritual goal.

C. *Refutation of Arguments Used by Far Eastern Religions to Support Their Position on Salvation*

1. Theravada Buddhism

   a. In essence, Theravadins believe that eliminating all desires is the only way to attain personal salvation.

   b. The major problem with this Theravadin doctrine is that the Theravadin is caught in a moral contradiction. Theravadins must put all of their effort and ambition into saving themselves, but the desire to seek after enlightenment (or *parinirvana* or salvation) is doing the very thing that prevents enlightenment.

   c. In Theravadin Buddhism, the focus of salvation is on the individual. All that a Theravadin monk or nun does is to save oneself. No one can do it for him or her. Likewise, what the Theravadin does helps no one else. Therefore, saving oneself is just as selfish as doing anything else for oneself.

   d. In fact, the Theravadin is so concerned with personal salvation that he or she abandons everything in order to pursue it. That is why the Theravadin must renounce the world, join a monastic order, and eliminate all desires.

   e. "Thus Buddhism is caught in a double bind," says David L. Johnson. "A person must want to be saved from selfishness to achieve enlightenment. But wanting to get saved is itself selfish. It is wanting something for oneself. This concern for personal salvation is the fundamental problem which prevents salvation."[66]

2. Zen Buddhism

   a. In Zen Buddhism, the obstacle to attaining satori (enlightenment) is thinking or rational thought. Therefore, Zen Buddhists believe that the solution is to have a "nonthinking" mind.

   b. The problem with this prescription for enlightenment is that Zen Buddhists employ a highly sophisticated technique (i.e., Zen meditation) to erase the mind of all beliefs and ideas.

   c. Technique itself consists of the application of shared knowledge to achieve step by step an agreed upon goal—that in itself constitutes cognitive thinking.

   d. Each day we use many techniques, such as programming a VCR, making coffee, or driving a car. Likewise, Zen meditation is a technique because it requires an understanding of *how to* achieve enlightenment. Therefore, rational thought must be used in order to understand how to do it.

---

[66]David L. Johnson, *A Reasoned Look at Asian Religions* (Minneapolis: Bethany House, 1985), 131.

e. In addition, the attempt to clear and empty the mind of any capacity to discriminate is to remove any ability to comprehend God, who reveals himself through rational thought. Stephen H. Short, a former Zen Buddhist, makes this point clear by saying, "Everything Zen had urged me to destroy was necessary in order to know God."[67]

3. Amida Buddhism

a. Amida Buddhists believe that the Amida will save them if they have a sincere faith in his infinite compassion.

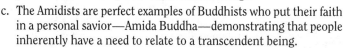

b. Although the Buddha taught that speculation about the divine hinders the attainment of enlightenment, many Buddhists pursue a personal relationship with supernatural beings.

c. The Amidists are perfect examples of Buddhists who put their faith in a personal savior—Amida Buddha—demonstrating that people inherently have a need to relate to a transcendent being.

d. Augustine described this hunger to know God by saying, "Thou hast formed us for Thyself, and our hearts are restless till they find rest in Thee."[68]

e. Therefore, Amidist faith in a personal savior indicates a fundamental weakness in the Buddha's teaching not to conjecture about God, which even devout and pious Buddhists, like the Amidists, cannot maintain.

f. Meanwhile, the problem for the Amida Buddhists is that their doctrine on faith has no support from the original teachings of the Buddha.

4. Nichiren Shoshu Buddhism

a. Chanting is the key to personal salvation for Nichiren Buddhists since they believe that chanting the daimoku is a repository of magical power, giving them both material and spiritual benefits.

b. The problem with this emphasis on the benefits of chanting is that it doesn't attract people who are concerned with detachment from all desires, which is basic to the Buddha's teaching, but attracts people who chant for things they want.

c. "The emphasis on materialism and the element of personal power," says John Weldon, "are the most obvious attractions of Nichiren Buddhism. . . . The philosophy underlying this idea is probably of little concern to most followers, who are satisfied to simply be receiving benefits."[69]

---

[67]Stephen H. Short, "Zen and the Art of Not Knowing God," *Christian Research Journal* (Winter/Spring 1990): 26.

[68]Augustine, *Confessions,* trans. F. J. Sheed (New York: Sheed &Ward, 1943), 3.

[69]John Weldon, "Nichiren Shoshu Buddhism," *Christian Research Journal* (Fall 1992): 11.

   d. In fact, despite Nichiren Buddhists' claim that they uniquely teach true Buddhism, Yale historian Kenneth Scott Latourette says that Nichiren "was mistaken in his conviction that the Lotus Sutra contained the primitive Buddhism. As a matter of fact, it was a late production, an expression of a form of Buddhism that would scarcely have been recognized by Gautama, or if recognized, would have been repudiated."[70]

   e. In short, Nichiren Shoshu Buddhism promotes a self-gratifying religion that is at cross-purposes with the Four Noble Truths of the Buddha.

5. Tibetan Buddhism

   a. Tibetan Buddhists employ occultic techniques with which to achieve personal salvation. Mystical aids assist Tibetan Buddhists in their spiritual quest. Of all the major Far Eastern religions, Tibetan Buddhism is arguably the one most steeped in spiritism.

   b. Concerning spiritism, Walter Martin states, "the Eternal God has condemned its practice in the sternest possible terms, maintaining that the interpretation of the supernatural realms belongs solely to him (Genesis 40:8), and that those who practice intrusion into these realms are worthy of death (Exodus 22:18)."[71]

   c. In addition, Tibetan Buddhists are dependent on the guidance of Tibetan spiritual masters. "In Tibetan Buddhism," says Marku Tsering, "all spiritual progress depends upon pleasing one's lama (or teacher)."[72]

   d. God's warning is clear: "Do not turn to mediums or seek out spiritists, for you will be defiled by them. I am the LORD your God" (Lev. 19:31).

6. Taoism

   a. The Taoist exalts nonactivity as a way to be in harmony with the Tao. "For human beings to intervene in any way with the laws of the universe is to upset the intricate balance of yin and yang."[73]

   b. "The harsh criticism leveled against Taoism by its opponents has long been that it is a religion that rejects human activity at every level, whether it be political, social, familial, or the like," says George A. Mather and Larry A. Nichols. In short, Taoism "reinforces laziness, noninvolvement, and apathy."[74]

   c. In addition, whether Taoists use esoteric techniques or try to live passively, they view discrimination (i.e., making distinctions) as a

---

[70]Kenneth Scott Latourette, *Introduction to Buddhism* (New York: Friendship Press, 1956), 38.

[71]Walter Martin, *The Kingdom of the Cults*, rev. ed. (Minneapolis: Bethany House, 1985), 233.

[72]Marku Tsering, "The Tibetan Buddhist World," *International Journal of Frontier Missions* 10, no. 3 (July 1993): 150.

[73]Mather and Nichols, *Dictionary of Cults, Sects, Religions, and the Occult*, 271.

[74]Ibid.

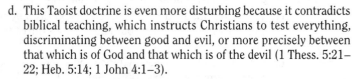
disruption of nature and thus try to avoid perceiving and behaving in dualistic terms.

d. This Taoist doctrine is even more disturbing because it contradicts biblical teaching, which instructs Christians to test everything, discriminating between good and evil, or more precisely between that which is of God and that which is of the devil (1 Thess. 5:21–22; Heb. 5:14; 1 John 4:1–3).

e. In fact, we are to "hate what is evil" and "cling to what is good" (Rom. 12:9). Clearly, this entails making moral distinctions.

7. Confucianism

a. Confucianists follow a moral, ethical code in order to bring peace and happiness to the individual and society.

b. "Reciprocity," which is at the heart of Confucianism, reflects both the strength and weakness of Confucian ethics. Emphasizing that we should not harm others is commendable and is certainly a biblical principle. And yet, the Bible goes further—it is not enough to avoid treating people badly, but we must always think about how we can minister to the needs of others (Luke 10:36–37; Rom. 15:1–2; Gal. 6:9–10; 1 John 3:17–18).

c. When Confucius said, "What you do not want done to yourself, do not do to others,"[75] he was instructing his followers to focus on themselves. "For Confucius," says C. George Fry, "self-love or self-respect was the first saving virtue. A man who honors himself will not dishonor another."[76]

d. When Jesus said, "In everything, do to others what you would have them do to you, for this sums up the Law and the Prophets" (Matt. 7:12), he was teaching his disciples to focus on others.

e. This then is the contrast between Confucianism and Christianity: in Confucianism, we behave ethically and morally for ourselves and society; in Christianity, we behave ethically and morally for others and for God.

D. Arguments Used to Prove the Biblical Doctrine of Salvation[77]

1. God's grace versus human works

a. We are saved by God's grace through faith in Christ (Eph. 2:8).

(1) God's grace is that Jesus Christ died on our behalf and atoned for our sins so that we might know God's forgiveness (Rom. 3:24–26).

---

[75]*Analects* 15:23.

[76]C. George Fry, et al., *Great Asian Religions,* 104.

[77]Almost all of the major Far Eastern religions teach that a person must earn his or her salvation (or the spiritual goal for which they are striving). The one exception is Amida Buddhism. Their belief in Amida Buddha as their savior will be refuted later under "The Doctrines of God" (V.C.3).

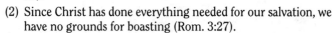

          (2) God's grace cannot be earned (Rom. 11:6; Gal. 2:21).

     b. We can contribute nothing to our salvation (Eph. 2:9).

          (1) We are not justified (i.e., declared "not guilty") by observing God's laws, but by putting our faith in Jesus Christ (Gal. 2:15–16).

          (2) Since Christ has done everything needed for our salvation, we have no grounds for boasting (Rom. 3:27).

     c. Though we are not saved *by* our good works, we are saved *in order to do* good works (Eph. 2:10).

          (1) Our good works demonstrate the genuineness of our faith in Christ (James 2:14, 18).

          (2) According to God's eternal plan, he is transforming us into the image of Jesus Christ (Rom. 8:29). In effect, God is the potter and we are the clay (Isa. 64:8; Jer. 18:6; Rom. 9:20).

          (3) Because true faith in Christ produces obedience, our good works are a result, not a cause, of God's work in us (Rom. 1:5; Phil. 2:12–13; 1 Thess. 1:3).

  2. Atonement in Jesus Christ

     a. During the early days of the Christian church, the apostle Peter made a public declaration that only through Jesus Christ can a person be saved (Acts 4:8–12).

     b. In fact, Jesus taught that he is the only way in which a person can be accepted by God (John 14:6).

V. The Doctrines of God

A. Major Far Eastern Positions on the Doctrine of God Briefly Stated

  1. Theravada Buddhism—Speculations about God hinders a person's pursuit for enlightenment.

  2. Zen Buddhism—No supreme being exists who can help a person experience satori (i.e., enlightenment).

  3. Amida Buddhism—Amida Buddha was a man who became a godlike being.

  4. Nichiren Buddhism—Nichiren was a Japanese Buddhist monk, who is worshiped as a Buddha.

  5. Tibetan Buddhism—Tantric deities are essential to Tibetan spiritual exercises.

  6. Taoism—The Tao is the Absolute and not any supreme being.

  7. Confucianism—Confucius intentionally avoided any discussion about heavenly beings in his teachings.

B. Arguments Used by Far Eastern Religions to Support Their Positions on the Doctrine of God

1. Theravada Buddhism

   a. Although some claim that original Buddhism was an atheistic religion because the Buddha did not instruct his followers to worship any deity, ancient Buddhist doctrines do not deny the existence of gods.

   b. In fact, the Buddha taught that the gods inhabit the cosmos and are impermanent like all other living beings. Thus, they too must escape rebirth through *parinirvana*.

   c. The Buddha discouraged the worship of any god or himself, but rather stressed the following of his teachings. Richard H. Robinson writes, "Gautama is reported to have said, 'What is there in seeing this wretched body? Whoever sees Dharma [his teaching] sees me; whoever sees me sees Dharma.' The immortality of the Buddha is that he is immanent in his Word."[78]

   d. Theravada Buddhism affirms that the Buddha was a teacher and not a god. "Among the founders of religions the Buddha," says Theravadin scholar Walpola Rahula, "was the only teacher who did not claim to be other than a human being, pure and simple." In fact, the Buddha "claimed no inspiration from any god or external power either. He attributed all his realization, attainments, and achievements to human endeavor and human intelligence."[79]

   e. Whether Theravadins maintain that the Buddha regarded the gods as only a concept or as inferior beings,[80] their belief is that any consideration of God is pointless.

2. Zen Buddhism

   a. In Buddhism, the Buddha (or Buddhas) is exalted above all other beings, including the gods (or God). However, even the Buddha is not the primary spiritual focus of Zen Buddhists, but rather their own Buddha nature.

   b. The Zen Buddhist must not look to the Buddha but know that he or she is a Buddha himself or herself. "For Buddha's sake," says D. T. Suzuki, "Buddha is to be given up. This is the only way to come to the realization of the truth of Zen."[81]

   c. "The Zen Buddhist," says Emma McCloy Layman, "is not required to have faith in any Buddha—in fact, he may spit upon a Buddha-image or curse the Buddha if he wishes. What he must have is faith

---

[78]Richard H. Robinson, *The Buddhist Religion* (Belmont, Calif.: Dickenson, 1970), 35.

[79]Walpola, *What the Buddha Taught*, 1.

[80]See Kalupahana, *Buddhist Philosophy*, 65–66.

[81]D. T. Suzuki, *An Introduction to Zen Buddhism* (New York: Grove Press, 1964), 54–55.

in his own Buddha-nature, and determination to persevere with zazen until and after he experiences satori."[82]

d. In short, Zen Buddhists maintain that any belief in the existence of a transcendent God is not only a false view of reality but also harmful to one's spiritual condition.

3. Amida Buddhism

   a. According to Amidist tradition,[83] incalculable aeons ago a king heard the teachings of a Buddha (not Gautama, but an earlier Buddha). After this king relinquished his kingdom and became a Buddhist monk, he assumed the name Dharmakara.

   b. He then devoted himself to practicing countless good deeds, and eventually he became the Amida Buddha. He currently dwells in a Western Paradise—a land of purity and happiness, where faithful believers in the Amida are reborn because of his compassion.

   c. "Amida is the saving Buddha, highly revered by Amidist sects," says E. Dale Saunders. "He is twofold in nature, the two aspects being apparent in his Sanskrit names: Amitayus, 'long life'; and Amitabha, 'limitless light.' . . . The outstanding quality of this divinity is his generosity toward the worshiper, whose every sin he forgives and whom he goes out to meet and welcome into his paradise."[84]

   d. Buddhists of the Pure Land schools, such as the Jodo Shinshu, worship Amida Buddha in churches and temples in North America. They also show their devotion to him at their Butsu-dan, a small Buddhist altar, which serves as a family shrine at the center of their home so that the Amida Buddha can purify the daily life of the family.

4. Nichiren Shoshu Buddhism

   a. Nichiren was a Japanese monk who lived in the thirteenth century. His teachings on the *Lotus Sutra* established a new school of Buddhism, which has a wide following worldwide, including about a half a million in North America.

   b. Although Nichiren Buddhists worship the *Gohonzon* (an inscription on wood of the prayer "*Namu myo-ho-renge-kyo*"), they place their personal faith in Nichiren, whom they believe was the incarnation of Jogyo, a bodhisattva (one who has achieved Buddhahood but delays *parinirvana* in order to help save others with his vast reservoir of good merits).

   c. Meanwhile, Nichiren Buddhists hold that the eternal Buddha is without beginning or end. While other Nichiren schools of Bud-

---

[82]Layman, *Buddhism in America*, 54–55.
[83]This version of the story about Amida is contained in the *Larger Sukhavati-vyuha*.
[84]Saunders, *Buddhism in Japan*, 168, 170.

dhism teach that Gautama was this Buddha, "in Nichiren Sho-shu, the Buddha is Nichiren himself (called Nichiren Dai-Shonin)."[85]

    d. In short, for Nichiren Shoshu Buddhists, Nichiren assumes multiple roles: as Jogyo, a bodhisattva, he is a divine savior; and as the supreme Buddha, he is the eternal god.

5. Tibetan Buddhism

    a. In Tibetan Buddhism, a pantheon of innumerable Buddhas, bodhisattvas, and their consorts are at the forefront of this religion. This can be seen in their icons, ceremonies, and teachings.

    b. Geshe Lobsang Tharchin explains how Buddhas link the divine with the human: "We should say a word here about these 'divine beings.' We Buddhists believe that there are many Buddhas in the universe.... We believe that a Buddha is the ultimate evolution of all life; that he can know all things, but does not have all power: he did not create the universe, for example.... nor can he take all our sufferings away from us by himself.... We do believe that by studying and practicing the teaching of the Buddha we ourselves can become Buddhas, as can every living being."[86]

    c. While worshiping the many divinities in their religion, on a temporal level Tibetan Buddhists pay homage to their spiritual teachers known as lamas. "Tibetan Buddhism took on the particular form of Lamaism from the very vital role of the 'lama' or priest-teacher, around whom religious activity centered," writes Laura Pilarski. "Lamaism developed into a complex and intricate system, with its own philosophical dialectics and metaphysics, its different aspects of yoga, its numerous rituals, popular traditions, literature, and systems of divination."[87]

    d. The most well-known lama is the Dalai Lama, who is the spiritual and temporal leader of Tibetan Buddhism. The current Dalai Lama is the fourteenth Dalai Lama, who Tibetan Buddhists believe is the reincarnation of the previous Dalai Lama. This succession of reincarnations can be traced back to the first Dalai Lama in the fifteenth century, who is believed to be the reincarnation of a bodhisattva.

    e. Thus Tibetan Buddhists venerate divine beings in the forms of Buddhas, bodhisattvas, and their earthly incarnations, such as the Dalai Lama.

6. Taoism

    a. Through the centuries, religious Taoism in Asia (primarily China) incorporated a hierarchy of cosmic forces into its belief system and

---

[85]N. S. Brannen, "Nichiren Buddhism," in *The Perennial Dictionary of World Religions*, 538.

[86]Geshe Lobsang Tharchin, "Foreword," in *Tsongkapa: The Principal Teachings of Buddhism* (Howell, N.J.: Classics of Middle Asia, 1988), 17.

[87]Laura Pilarski, *Tibet: Heart of Asia* (Indianapolis: Bobbs-Merrill, 1974), 27.

63

religious ceremonies. A vast bureaucracy of gods and goddesses evolved, with the Tao still perceived as *the* preeminent force in the universe.

b. Philosophical Taoism, however, has been primarily concerned with understanding how the Tao underlines the basic principles of nature, not with countenancing any formalized worship of deities. In the West, people are more familiar with and exposed to philosophical Taoism rather than religious Taoism.

c. "For the Taoists," says H. G. Creel, "they used the term *Tao* to stand for the totality of all things, equivalent to what some Western philosophers have called 'the absolute.' The *Tao* was the basic stuff out of which all things were made. It was simple, formless, desireless, without striving, supremely content. It existed before Heaven and Earth. In the course of the generation of things and institutions, the farther man gets away from this primal state, the less good, and the less happy, he is."[88]

d. Therefore, the goal of the Taoist is to become one with the Tao, which, as Arthur Waley suggests, is experienced as a "road, path, way."[89]

e. Although Taoists argue that the Tao cannot be defined in words, it can be said that Taoists view the Tao as the primal, impersonal essence of the natural world.

7. Confucianism

a. Although "Confucius claimed no divine revelation"[90] nor special insight into the nature of God and the heavenly realm, he did note that his ethical teachings were in accord with the ways of heaven.[91]

b. Over time a cult of Confucius emerged in China. These Confucianists built temples, offered sacrifices to Confucius, and venerated ancestral spirits.

c. In A.D. 59, Emperor Han Ming Ti recognized Confucius as patron of scholars, and shortly afterward, Confucianism became the official state religion.

d. The cult of Confucius continued until the twentieth century when communism and other modern developments in China put an end to rituals in which sacrifices were offered to Confucius.

e. Nevertheless, Confucian ethics still influence the conduct of the Chinese and other Asian peoples.

f. Meanwhile, Confucian philosophy leaves the doctrine of God to the theology of other religions.

---

[88]H. G. Creel, *Chinese Thought from Confucius to Mao Tse-tung* (New York: A Mentor Book, 1953), 87.
[89]Arthur Waley, *The Way and Its Power* (London: Allen and Unwin, 1956), 30.
[90]C. George Fry, et al., *Great Asian Religions,* 88.
[91]*Analects* 2:4.

C. Refutation of Arguments Used by Far Eastern Religions to Support Their Positions on the Doctrine of God

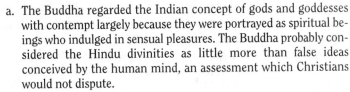

1. Theravada Buddhism

   a. The Buddha regarded the Indian concept of gods and goddesses with contempt largely because they were portrayed as spiritual beings who indulged in sensual pleasures. The Buddha probably considered the Hindu divinities as little more than false ideas conceived by the human mind, an assessment which Christians would not dispute.

   b. The Buddha and Theravadins, however, not only dismiss Vishnu, Siva, and Krishna, but also all gods, including Yahweh—the one true God. Refusing to acknowledge the lordship of God the Father and Christ his Son strikes at the heart of the Christian faith.

   c. Throughout the Bible, people are told to acknowledge God and his ways. "Trust in the LORD with all your heart and lean not on your own understanding; in all your ways acknowledge him, and he will make your paths straight" (Prov. 3:5–6).

   d. Indeed, God demands that we acknowledge him and his power (Isa. 33:13; Hos. 6:3), and if we do acknowledge him and Jesus as our Lord, he will save us because of his great love for us (Ps. 91:14–16; Matt. 10:32; Luke 12:8; Rom. 10:9; 1 John 4:15–16).

   e. Furthermore, Christian theologians argue effectively that God exists in three persons, as the Bible proclaims.[92] Their arguments refute not only atheism but Theravada statements about God.

2. Zen Buddhism

   a. Like the Theravadins, Zen Buddhists reject the belief in the existence of a transcendent God. In fact, they assert that such a belief chains a person to a false understanding of the Absolute and obstructs that person from realizing his or her Buddha nature and attaining satori (enlightenment).

   b. "For traditional Christianity, TRANSCENDENCE and IMMANENCE both comprise the triune God who is Father, Son, and Holy Spirit," says George A. Mather and Larry A. Nichols. "Such a notion of a personal, providential, and salvific God is inimical to the mind of the Zen Buddhist."[93]

   c. While denying God, Zen Buddhists believe they are Buddhas themselves. Though few of them would make such a statement, in effect they view themselves as god.

---

[92]For arguments affirming the existence of God and the doctrine of the trinity, see Millard Erickson, *God in Three Persons: A Contemporary Interpretation of the Trinity* (Grand Rapids: Baker, 1985), and J. P. Moreland and Kai Nielsen, *Does God Exist? The Debate between Theists and Atheists* (Buffalo: Prometheus Books, 1993).

[93]Mather and Nichols, *Dictionary of Cults, Sects, Religions, and the Occult,* 327.

    d. The God of the Bible has harsh words for people who exalt themselves above him and deny his preeminence.

        (1) Those who seek to be like "the Most High" will be brought down to the depths of the pit (Isa. 14:13–15).

        (2) Those who magnify themselves above God and deride him will come to an end (Dan. 11:36–37, 45b).

        (3) Pride deceives their heart into thinking that nothing can bring them down from the heights, but God will bring them down (Obad. 3–4).

        (4) They are like the leader of the forces of evil, who proclaims himself to be God while opposing and exalting himself above everything of God (2 Thess. 2:3–4; see Rev. 13:6).

        (5) Indeed, Jesus will overthrow and destroy the evil one and those whom the evil one has deceived (2 Thess. 2:8–12).

  3. Amida Buddhism

    a. Since Gautama discouraged his followers from worshiping him, Amidists evidently conceived of a god to whom they could pay homage. Because Amidists believe that Amida was a human being whose earthly existence was countless aeons ago, and because the Amidists cannot supply documents contemporary with Amida's earthly existence to prove that he was a historical figure, the Amida Buddha must be considered a myth.

    b. Over time, Amidists have provided Amida with an earthly history and have worshiped him as a savior god. The problem with Amidism is that it teaches a faith in a personal god who has no verifiable personal history.

    c. In contrast to Amida Buddhism, however, Christianity places its faith in a historical figure—Jesus Christ—whose existence both Christians and non-Christians verify.

    d. Of course, the Bible affirms the historicity of Jesus Christ.

        (1) It provides Jesus' partial biography, even denoting his exact time in human history (Luke 2:1; 3:1–2).

        (2) While Paul spoke against those who devote themselves to myths (1 Tim. 1:4), his fellow believers, Peter and John, claimed that they were actual eyewitnesses of Christ, and even touched him (2 Peter 1:16; 1 John 1:1–2).

        (3) Even after his death and after he rose from the dead, Jesus told his followers to touch him and know that he had flesh and bones (Luke 24:39).

    e. Meanwhile, non-Christians also provide written sources for our knowledge of the life and teaching of Jesus Christ.

        (1) The earliest non-Christian witness to the historicity of Jesus Christ is the Jewish historian, Flavius Josephus, who lived in

the first century A.D. In the *Antiquities of the Jews,* Josephus referred to Christ's teachings, marvelous deeds, and death on the cross (xviii.iii.3).

(2) The Babylonian Talmud is a collection of Jewish traditions, which were written down in the fifth century and go as far back as the first century. Though hostile to Jesus, they show that he lived, did miracles, and made definite claims about his divine status. For example, it indicates that Jesus performed miracles (though they attribute them to magic); that Jesus indeed claimed to be God (which they cite as proof of his apostasy); and that Jesus was an illegitimate child (in contradiction to the biblical account of his virgin birth). The fact that these witnesses are *hostile* to Jesus actually enhances their value in establishing the historicity of what Jesus did and said, since the authors could hardly be charged with trying to advance belief in Christ.

(3) The earliest Latin author who refers to Christ is Pliny the Younger. Pliny wrote about Christians singing hymns to Christ (*Epist.* x.96, written about A.D. 112).

(4) The Roman historian Tacitus mentions that Pontius Pilate condemned Christ to death (*Annals,* xv. 44, written about A.D. 115). Says New Testament scholar Bruce M. Metzger, "The importance of this pagan testimony to the historicity of Christ is hard to exaggerate. Tacitus is universally acknowledged to be one of the most reliable of Roman historians, whose passion for sober and accurate reporting was joined with a critical sense rare in his time. It is significant that he fixes the date of Jesus' death in terms of the reigning emperor as well as the procurator of Judea."[94]

(5) Suetonius briefly refers to Christ in chapter 25 of the *Lives of the Twelve Caesars* (published about A.D. 120).

(6) Metzger makes this comment about these non-Christian references to Jesus Christ: "The early non-Christian testimonies concerning Jesus, though scanty, are sufficient to prove (even without taking into account the evidence contained in the New Testament) that he was a historical figure who lived in Palestine in the early years of the first century, that he gathered a group of followers about himself, and that he was condemned to death under Pontius Pilate. Today no competent scholar denies the historicity of Jesus."[95]

4. Nichiren Shoshu Buddhism

   a. Nichiren Shoshu Buddhists worship the *Gonhonzon* (an inscrip-

---

[94]Bruce M. Metzger, *The New Testament: Its Background, Growth, and Content* (New York: Abingdon, 1965), 77.

[95]Ibid., 78.

tion of a Buddhist prayer on wood or paper). They also venerate Nichiren, whom they exalt above God.

b. Worshiping the *Gonhonzon,* however, is idol worship, which God emphatically forbids (Ex. 20:3–5). Furthermore, Jesus rebuked pagan babbling such as chanting *Namu myo-ho-renge-kyo* repeatedly (Matt. 6:7). The Bible also says that there is no profit or value in worshiping idols made out of wood, for only God is God (Isa. 44:6, 9–10, 15, 19; Hab. 2:18–19; 1 Cor. 8:4–6).

c. Although Nichiren was a historical figure like Jesus, the Bible teaches that Jesus Christ is the only mediator between God the Father and human beings (1 Tim. 2:5). Moreover, the apostle Peter affirmed that people can be saved only through Jesus Christ (Acts 4:10, 12). Indeed, Jesus himself said that no one can approach God the Father except through him (John 14:6).

5. Tibetan Buddhism

a. A pantheon of innumerable gods and goddesses is central to the beliefs and rituals in Tibetan Buddhism. In fact, the spiritual goal of Tibetan Buddhists is to become one of these Buddhas or bodhisattvas, which really is seeking to become like a god.

b. This sophisticated form of polytheism is idolatry, which the Bible clearly condemns and which Christians should denounce. "The initial step in the conversion of Buddhists is a cessation of idol worship and spirit veneration," says Tissa Weerasingha. "The cessation of idol worship is a sign that there is a realization of the powerlessness of 'gods' against the supremacy of Christ."[96]

c. In short, invoking supernatural beings and serving them, which Tibetan Buddhists do, are offenses to Yahweh (Ex. 23:13, 33; Deut. 6:14; 11:28; Josh. 24:16; Judg. 10:13; 2 Chron. 33:1–4; Jer. 35:15; 1 Cor. 8:5–6). Indeed, these gods are not gods at all (Jer. 2:11; Gal. 4:8), for there is no god except Yahweh (2 Sam. 7:22; Eph. 4:6).

d. In addition, the spiritual dynamics of how Tibetan Buddhists and Christians relate to evil spiritual entities also illustrate a striking difference between the two religions. "In Buddhism, spirits and demonic powers are appeased," says Paul Wagner, "in Scripture they are resisted and cast out."[97]

e. Finally, the desire to become like God (in the wrong way) was a major reason why the first woman disobeyed God (Gen. 3:5), which led to humanity's estrangement from God.

(1) Here is what God says to those who seek to seize what is rightfully his: "In the pride of your heart you say, 'I am a god; I sit

---

[96]Tissa Weerasingha, "Karma and Christ," *International Journal of Frontier Missions* 10, no. 3 (July 1993): 104.

[97]Paul Wagner, "Taking the High Places for God," *International Journal of Frontier Missions* 10, no. 3 (July 1993): 98.

on the throne of a god in the heart of the seas.' But you are a man and not a god, though you think you are as wise as a god" (Ezek. 28:2).

(2) God will surely bring down those who try to make themselves elevated like God—even unto hell (Isa. 14:14–15).

(3) Whereas Buddhists strive for Buddhahood, Christians practice servanthood (Rom. 14:18; Gal. 5:13; Eph. 4:11–13; 1 Tim. 3:13; Heb. 9:14).

6. Taoism

a. Taoists perceive the Tao as the Absolute. The Tao is said to be the Way, the Truth, the Path. Taoists do not believe the Tao is a personal god, but a primal force that pervades the natural world.

b. When the apostle Paul informed the Athenians that the God who made the world and gave life to every man and woman will also judge the world with justice (Acts 17:22–31), Paul was telling the Greeks that God can be known to them because he is personal. Indeed, if we are made in "the image of God" (Gen. 1:27), can God be less personal than his creation?

c. Not only can we know God, but also God *knows* us (Gal. 4:9; see also 1 Sam. 2:3). In fact, God has a mind (Rom. 11:34), which an impersonal force cannot have.

d. Furthermore, God often communicated with humans. He spoke to Adam and Eve in Eden (Gen. 3:9–19) and to Moses on Mount Horeb (Ex. 3:4–4:17). He spoke to Peter, John, and James when Jesus was transfigured, saying that he *loved* his Son (Matt. 17:5; Mark 9:7; Luke 9:35). Each event shows God's personal nature. In fact, everyone who listens to God can be "taught by God" (John 6:45). Can impersonality teach?

e. Paul also made the point that there is "One God and Father of all, who is over all and through all and in all" (Eph. 4:6). Not only is God transcendent and immanent, but also he is Father, the most intimate reference to God as a personal being.

(1) Indeed, throughout the Bible, God is said to be Father (Deut. 32:6; Ps. 2:7; Isa. 63:16; Mal. 2:10; Matt. 5:16; 6:9, 26; 18:10; Luke 23:34; etc.).

(2) Jesus emphasized the fatherhood of God in many of his parables, especially the parable of the lost son (Luke 15:11–32), and as the personal being we address in prayer (Matt. 6:9–13).

(3) In addition, in Ephesians 3:14–15, Paul implied that all persons designated as human fathers derive their fatherhood from a personal heavenly Father.

f. In discussing the theological difference between Taoism and Christianity, Mather and Nichols point out that "Christianity maintains that far from being an impersonal force [Tao], God is personal in Jesus Christ."[98]

(1) When Jesus said, "I and the Father are one" (John 10:30), he made it clear that we can know the personal God by knowing Christ who is personal (John 17:3).

(2) In fact, instead of the Tao being "the Way," Jesus said in answer to the question: "How can we know the way?" "I am the way and the truth and the life" (John 14:5–6).

7. Confucianism

a. Confucius seldom spoke about God and the heavenly realm, but when he did, he did with respect.

b. "The sage's silence on the supernatural derived from his lack of knowledge on the subject," says C. George Fry. "A key virtue for the ideal man [in Confucianism] is truthfulness. When one knows not, one ought not speak. . . ." Accordingly, "Confucius denied having an experiential knowledge of the spiritual realm."[99]

c. On this basis and in this area, we can agree with David L. Johnson, who says, "Confucian theory is difficult to criticize." Nevertheless, Confucianism "never realized the ideal order that it preached."[100]

d. Despite the high moral ethics of Confucian teachings, it is still powerless apart from the power of God to transform human character. Confucianism may be admirable as far as it can humanly go, but unless one is found by the divine, one is still lost forever.

D. Arguments Used to Prove the Biblical Doctrine on God

1. Being triune, God subsists eternally in three persons: the Father, the Son, and the Holy Spirit.

a. Matthew illustrated the distinction of the three persons of the godhead in his record of Jesus' baptism, when the Holy Spirit descended upon Jesus and the Father spoke to him from heaven (Luke 3:21–22).

b. At the last supper, Jesus said he had come from the Father and was returning to the Father (John 16:28). Jesus also said the Holy Spirit (the Counselor) could not come to his disciples until he had returned to heaven. Thus Jesus taught that he, God the Father, and the Holy Spirit are personally distinct from one another.

c. Paul said, "May the grace of the Lord Jesus Christ, and the love of God, and the fellowship of the Holy Spirit be with you all." This verse has been the trinitarian benediction used in Christian worship to acknowledge the full equality of the Holy Spirit.

---

[98]Mather and Nichols, *Dictionary of Cults, Sects, Religions, and the Occult,* 271.

[99]C. George Fry, et al., *Great Asian Religions,* 101.

[100]David L. Johnson, *A Reasoned Look at Asian Religions,* 41.

    d. John said, "the Word [Jesus] was *with* God [the Father], and the Word *was* God" (emphasis added); that is, Jesus and the Father are distinct persons who share the same essence.

2. Unity exists among the three persons of God; that is, the three persons are the one God.

    a. Paul said there is one God (Eph. 4:4–6).

    b. Jesus Himself recited the *Shema* (the Jewish confession of faith in the one true God from Deut. 6:4).

3. Jesus Christ is God.

    a. John called Jesus Christ the Word and the Word is God (John 1:1).

    b. Peter referred to Jesus Christ as his "God and Savior" (2 Peter 1:1).[101]

    c. Paul declared that all the fullness of the Deity dwells in Jesus Christ's bodily form (Col. 2:9; see also Rom. 9:5).

    d. He also called Jesus Christ his "great God" (Titus 2:13).[102]

    e. Upon believing in Jesus' bodily resurrection, Thomas called Jesus his Lord and God (John 20:28).

    f. At one time some Jews picked up rocks to stone Jesus because they thought he claimed to be God (John 10:33); Jesus made no effort to refute their belief.

    g. Even the Father called his Son "God" (Heb. 1:8).

---

[101]The Granville Sharp rule applies to 2 Peter 1:1 and Titus 2:13, which argues that "God" and "Savior" both have Jesus as the same referent: "When the copulative *kai* connects two nouns of the same case, if the article *ho* or any of its cases precedes the first of the said nouns or participles, and is not repeated before the second noun or participle, the latter always relates to the same person that is expressed or described by the first noun or participle; i.e., it denotes a farther description of the first-named person" (H. E. Dana and Julius R. Mantey, *A Manual Grammar of the Greek New Testament* [New York: MacMillan, 1927], 147).

[102]Ibid.

 **Part III:**
Witnessing Tips

I. Theravada Buddhists

A. *Their Identity*

1. Most Theravada Buddhists in North America are first- or second-generation Southeast Asian Americans.[1] This group includes both priests and laypersons.

2. Most Southeast Asian Americans who regard themselves as Theravada Buddhists are not learned students of their religion. Rather, they possess an elementary understanding of Buddhist doctrines and are more concerned with the religious rituals peculiar to their own cultural customs, which have been heavily influenced by ancient animistic beliefs.

3. Therefore, Christians should consider the cultural distinctives of the person with whom they are sharing their faith, the depth of that person's devotion to the Buddhist faith, and the intelligence of the person in so far as he or she can comprehend doctrinal and spiritual concepts.

B. *Evangelistic Suggestions*[2]

1. Consider language difficulties.

   a. Many first-generation Southeast Asian Americans are still learning English. Naturally, one must converse with them as simply as possible. But even the second generation, who are fluent in English, will not have been exposed to Christian doctrines enough to have a clue as to the meaning of words like atonement, sanctification, and resurrection.

   b. Christian concepts must be described to them in terms appropriate to their experiences, intelligence, and education. Christians should avoid theological abstractions, but instead illustrate their message with personal stories about sin, forgiveness, and God's love. Casting Jesus' parables into Southeast Asian American cultural experiences can be marvelously effective.

---

[1] A high percentage of North Americans who trace their ethnic roots to Southeast Asia are Vietnamese. These people can be classified into two religious groups: (1) Roman Catholics and (2) Mahayana Buddhists influenced by a strong element of Confucianism.

[2] These suggestions first appeared in my article, "The Arrival of Theravada: Southeast Asians Bring Their School of Buddhism to America," *Christian Research Journal* (Fall 1994): 38, 40.

(1) Rice is a daily staple of Southeast Asian Americans. Many of them are familiar with how this crop is harvested. Casting the parable of the sower and soils (Matt. 13:3–8, 18–43; Mark 4:3–8, 14–20; Luke 8:5–8, 11–15) in a setting familiar to these people, one can make the same comparisons and points even by saying that the seeds are rice seeds and the soils are paddies. In fact, they would probably have a better appreciation for this parable and other agricultural parables than most Americans would have, especially the parable of the tenants (Matt. 21:33–44; Mark 12:1–11; Luke 20:9–18) in which a vineyard can be changed to a rice paddy.

(2) If a Southeast Asian is still unmarried at thirty years of age or older, many Southeast Asians view that person as having brought dishonor to his or her family. A Christian can cast such a person as the Samaritan in the parable of the good Samaritan (Luke 10:30–37) and illustrate Jesus' point quite effectively.

c. Christians need to be aware that certain religious terms or phrases that have one meaning in a Christian setting can have an entirely different meaning to people of a different religious heritage.

(1) Tissa Weersingha, a Christian scholar and pastor in Sri Lanka, illustrates this point extremely well: "If a Buddhist were to be asked, 'Do you want to be born again?' he might likely reply, 'Please, no! I do NOT want to be born again. I want to reach nirvana.' The Buddhist quest is for deliverance from the cycle of rebirths. If a Buddhist confuses 'new birth' with 'rebirth,' the Christian message will be completely distorted."[3]

(2) Thus, avoid unexplained Christian clichés.

2. Distinguish between nirvana and heaven.

a. Theravadins hope that if they live a good enough life, they will be reborn to a more holy life than the one they presently live, and that finally, after a life as a Buddhist saint, they will experience nirvana—in which they will cease to exist altogether. Meanwhile, Christians have the assurance that they will be raised from the dead and enjoy eternal fellowship with Christ in his heavenly kingdom.

b. It might seem incredible that people would cling to the hope of nothingness while rejecting the promise of immortality with a loving God, but the fact is that many do. Attachment to family traditions, present earthly pursuits, and disbelief in such a God as Christ obscure how much better the Christian hope is.

---

[3]Tissa Weersingha, "Karma and Christ," *International Journal of Frontier Missions,* 10 (July 1993): 103.

   c. It should be noted that most Southeast Asian Americans do not see a difference between biblical principles and the American lifestyle.

     (1) For instance, it is difficult for them to understand the biblical view of God's heavenly kingdom when so many American Christians are heavily invested in living a prosperous life in this world.

     (2) We need to make clear the distinction between the lifestyle to which the Bible has called us and the lifestyle that too many of us have embraced in this world.

     (3) In recognizing this disparity, we can admit that some of us have fallen short but declare that others are being true to God's calling. Point to clear examples of Christians who have sacrificially dedicated their lives to Christ.

3. Be prepared for spiritual warfare.

   a. Christians must also recognize that when they share the Gospel with Southeast Asian Americans, they become engaged with spiritual warfare.

     (1) Certainly, conflict with evil always exists, especially when we evangelize.

     (2) In evangelizing these peoples, however, spiritual warfare is particularly intense since they participate in idol worship, the veneration of the spirits of deceased ancestors, and ceremonial rituals for the purpose of appeasing evil spirits.

   b. The Christian message is that we need not fear evil. Instead of appeasing these spirits, we can confidently resist them in Christ, who boldly cast them out during his earthly ministry.

     (1) Christ's victory over evil spirits is frequently displayed in the Gospels, and the Christian should often point out these passages to Southeast Asian Americans to assure them of this truth.

     (2) "Dear friends," said the apostle John, "do not believe every spirit, but test the spirits to see whether they are from God, because many false prophets have gone out into the world.... You, dear children, are from God and have overcome them, because the one who is in you is greater than the one who is in the world" (1 John 4:1, 4).

     (3) Thus we should pray that God will bind these demons from their lives and show them that God's people have no need to fear evil spirits because the love of Christ is greater than any other force (Rom. 8:38–39).

II. Zen Buddhists

A. *Their Identity*

1. Almost all of the Zen masters who live in North America are Asians, primarily from Japan or Korea. Meanwhile, a majority of laypersons who practice Zen in North America are Westerners of European descent.

   a. While Zendos (Zen centers) have been formed throughout North America, it is extremely difficult for an American to be officially recognized as a Zen master by Zen institutions in Japan or Korea. (The most notable exception is Philip Kapleau.)

   b. Thus most Westerners who practice Zen meditation are either living in a Zendo and studying under an Asian Zen teacher or are informally associated with a Zen organization and usually meditate on their own.

2. Many non-Asian Westerners are attracted to Zen because it is experience-oriented. Since North Americans place a high premium on experience, a number of people regard Zen as the vehicle that will transport them to that ultimate experience.

3. A high percentage of these people are college-educated, middle class, and suburban. They are generally self-reliant, individualistic, and attracted to the aesthetics of non-Western cultures.

B. *Evangelistic Suggestions*[4]

1. Since "nonthinking" is a vital element in Zen Buddhism, any attempt to argue religious doctrines invariably stalls as the Zen Buddhist discounts conceptual reasoning.

   a. This mind-set effectively blinds Zen Buddhists to the illogical implications of their assumptions about ultimate reality.

   b. Thus, when we engage in a religious dialogue with Zen Buddhists, we should avoid getting entangled in long discussions in which we try to persuade them that they must accept the logic of our argument.

2. Ultimately, the best route to the soul of most Zen Buddhists is not through their minds but through their hearts. Once the Holy Spirit touches their hearts, their minds will also be awakened to the truth of the Gospel. One way to accomplish this is to ask them a series of questions about different aspects of their faith in Zen. The benefit of querying is threefold:

   a. First, since Zen Buddhists are familiar with this mode of dialogue, they become more willing to address theological issues.

---

[4]These suggestions first appeared in my article, "Zest for Zen: North Americans Adopt This Meditative School of Buddhism," *Christian Research Journal* (Winter 1995): 8–15.

b. Second, it lays the cards faceup on the table for both sides to see—for them to recognize the implications of what they believe and for you to determine the weaknesses of their faith.

c. Third, it plants seeds of doubt that may later compel them to question the validity of their commitment to Zen.

3. In most cases when conversion has occurred, the Holy Spirit used evangelism primarily as a tool to dismantle the props that support the Zen Buddhist's attachment to nonthinking.

a. Therefore, just getting Zen Buddhists to think about what they believe is often a giant step in opening their hearts to the Gospel, which normally occurs later when they struggle with the Lord privately.

b. Of course, it is useless—perhaps even mean-spirited—to attempt to crush a person's faith and not offer something better in its place, which, of course, is Jesus Christ.

c. After asking them questions about a certain point, we can share what we believe about that point, constantly resisting the urge to argue. Then we can go on to the next point. If they ask questions about our faith, then we can address specific issues more thoroughly. In this way we will plant not only seeds of doubt but seeds of hope as well.

d. For areas to discuss with Zen Buddhists, examine the doctrinal sections in this book on the soul, self-effort, and detachment. These subjects provide the most fruitful areas for discussion and in sharing the Christian faith.

III. Amida Buddhists

A. *Their Identity*

1. Most Amida Buddhists in North America are Japanese Americans who belong to Shodo Shinshu Buddhism. They are members of the Buddhist Church of America. As more and more of these people marry outside their ethnic group, other peoples are joining this religion.

2. In many ways Japanese Americans have adapted their Buddhist religion to their Western environment.

a. For example, they often call their Buddhist temples "churches." Whereas in Japan Buddhists go to the temple any day of the week to worship, Japanese Americans "attend church" on Sunday mornings, and they even have Sunday schools.

b. Thus it is important to recognize that Shodo Shinshu Buddhism in North America is cross-cultural in many ways.

3. Like Westerners in North America who call themselves "Christians," Buddhists of the Amida faith can be classified as either devout or

nominal. Naturally, how you share the Gospel with a Japanese-American Buddhist will differ, depending in part on whether that person is devout or nominal.

    a. How will you be able to distinguish between the two groups? You won't unless you first develop a friendship with them.

    b. Friendship is a vital key in effective evangelism with them because Asians place a premium on long-lasting relationships.

B. *Evangelistic Suggestions*[5]

Understanding how certain characteristics affect Japanese Americans will not only help Christians build friendships with them, but will also provide us with insights in how to share the Gospel with them more effectively.

  1. The characteristic of *indebtedness*

    a. Many Japanese Americans feel indebted to anyone who does them a favor, gives them help, or acts kindly toward them. Of course, other people have this same compulsion to reciprocate, but this feeling is especially instilled in the thinking of Japanese Americans.

    b. Therefore, go out of your way to do something for them, and keep doing things for them. This may sound like manipulation, and if your motivation *is* to manipulate, then the results will be disastrous when they realize that you are doing these things only to proselytize them.

    c. If you sincerely want to become friends, however, it is important that you take the first step since many of them are naturally shy. They prefer to stand back and see what you do. If you treat them right, they will warm up to you with open arms.

  2. The characteristic of *shame*

    a. Shame and guilt are human qualities natural to all people. For whatever reason, however, shame seems to play a much more prominent role in affecting people of Asian descent than does guilt. Perhaps it is because Asian Americans are much more group-conscious than other Americans, who admire individualism.

    b. Many Asian Americans possess misgivings about identifying themselves with Christ because he died shamefully and dishonorably on the cross. First, they need to realize that only a god who suffered as Christ did can identify with their inner torments. Second, they need to realize that only a god who really cares for them would allow himself to be cruelly afflicted. Last, they need to realize that only a god who *truly is* God could rise from the tomb and give eternal life to those who believe in him.

---

[5]These suggestions first appeared in my three-part series "Sharing Your Faith with Asian Americans," *Christian Research Journal* (Summer 1992): 7; (Fall 1992): 7; (Winter 1993): 7.

c. While forming a relationship with a Japanese American, or any Asian American, it is important to remember that you are likely dealing with a person who makes decisions and behaves according to what his or her group—and particularly family—thinks and feels about something. In some cases, the family may believe that a particular member may be bringing shame on the family if he or she becomes a Christian. Although we shouldn't overaccommodate the wishes of the family, we need to take the extra step in being sensitive to a person's family. Perhaps then the whole household will become believers.

3. The characteristic of *"saving face"*

a. One of the most difficult considerations Christians need to understand while sharing the Gospel with Japanese Americans is the Asian concept of "saving face." What saving face really comes down to is refusing to admit when one is wrong. Of course, this tendency is not unique to Asian Americans, and there are Asian Americans who will freely confess their mistakes. Nevertheless, this kind of pride can be an important factor when we share our Christian faith with some Japanese Americans.

b. When Christians encounter this kind of pride in otherwise responsive Asian Americans, many Christians either argue that they must repent of their sins and stubborn pride if they want to become Christians, or they ignore the issue of repentance altogether. Both approaches are wrong.

c. A better way of teaching the importance of repentance of sins and public confession of faith in Christ is committing time and energy in studying the Bible with them and discussing from personal experience what certain Christian doctrines mean to you. But you can only have this kind of study after you become friends. And if you do, in time you may be blessed with gaining a dear brother or sister in Christ.

IV. Nichiren Shoshu Buddhists

A. *Their Identity*

1. A large majority both of leaders and of lay members in Nichiren Shoshu Buddhism (NSB) are non-Asians. Although NSB was primarily introduced to Japanese-American communities, NSB has since found its greatest success among affluent, white and black Americans.

2. Members of Nichiren Shoshu Buddhists are a close-knit group. Furthermore, of all the major Buddhist groups in North America, NSB is most noted for being on a mission to convert the world, which compels them to be further united in their dedication to the organization and to one another.

3. Although promotion of Nichiren Shoshu Buddhism tries to appeal to people of different religious backgrounds by being amicable to all beliefs, internally they are quite critical of other religions, even of other branches of Buddhism. They are particularly hostile toward Christian doctrines.

B. *Evangelistic Suggestions*

1. Since proselytizing is vigorously promoted in Nichiren Shoshu Buddhism, Christians have a unique opportunity in being able to dialogue with members of this Buddhist school that is not necessarily available with other Buddhists.

   a. Although their goal in wanting to talk with you is to convert you to their religion, and although they have probably been taught that Christianity is doctrinally flawed and ethically hypocritical, they are at least willing to discuss the merits and defects of both religions.

   b. Therefore, be biblically prepared to respond to their charges that it is foolish to believe people cannot save themselves, that Christian morality has caused evil and suffering in the world, and that Jesus could neither be a god nor a savior since he was executed on a cross.

2. Since personal happiness is a major concern of Nichiren Shoshu Buddhists, Christians should be cautious about being drawn into lengthy discussions about which religion offers true happiness.

   a. Christians certainly should not avoid describing the abiding joy and peace of being in Christ. However, if the central focus of the dialogue is on the difference between Buddhist happiness and serenity and Christian joy and peace, discussions are often drawn away from what it truly means to be under the lordship of Jesus Christ—perhaps even giving a false impression as to what it means to be a Christian.

   b. Even if frankness about the Christian faith causes them to reject the Gospel, Christians need to be up front about the judgment of God and the cost of being a disciple of Christ. In some cases, their rejection of the Gospel later produces an unwavering commitment to Christ because they have truly understood what it means to be a Christian.

3. Since Nichiren Shoshu Buddhists aggressively push their own religion, have a low view of Christianity, and emphasize worldly values, you may have more difficulty being loving toward this group of Buddhists. Thus, pray for God to empower you with Christ's love to be patient, sensitive, and loving toward them despite what they may say to you about Christianity.

V. Tibetan Buddhists

A. *Their Identity*

1. After communist China conquered Tibet in 1951, about 100,000 Tibetans fled their homeland because the communists treated the Tibetan people with extreme cruelty.

   a. Initially, the Tibetan exiles went to India, but many of them have since come to the West.

   b. These exiles include both religious leaders (such as the Dalai Lama and other lamas) and the laity.

2. Most importantly, as missionary Marku Tsering points out, "Many Tibetan Buddhist peoples see Buddhism as a rallying point for cultural survival. An individual who seriously considers religious change becomes open to charges of treason and social betrayal."[6]

3. Meanwhile, a number of Westerners of European descent not only have converted to Tibetan Buddhism, but also have adopted Tibetan customs, such as dress, food, and even speech patterns. Some have become lamas themselves. One example is Lama Anagarika Govinda.

B. *Evangelistic Suggestions*

1. Since the communists have ruthlessly tried to exterminate the Tibetan culture—particularly their religion—for nearly half a century, it is important for Christians to understand why Tibetans are extremely resistant to what they perceive as Christian attacks against their religion and cultural identity.

   a. On the one hand, we should be careful not to offend their cultural sensibilities. We should show them respect and be polite when we articulate the Gospel to them.

   b. On the other hand, we should not be so cautious to avoid upsetting them that we ignore presenting the Gospel to them altogether.

2. As with Southeastern Buddhists, Christians will be more effective in their evangelism of Tibetan Buddhists if they try to learn as much as possible about Tibetan culture and religion.

   a. Tsering makes the following astute comment about Christian missions to Tibetan Buddhists in Asia: "Missions conducted in ignorance of key Buddhist beliefs about suffering, sin, and redemption can run afoul of unintended meanings."[7]

   b. This statement is also true of evangelism of Tibetan Buddhists in North America.

---

[6]Marku Tsering, "The Tibetan Buddhist World," *International Journal of Frontier Missions* 10 (July 1993): 150.

[7]Ibid.

3. As for Westerners who have become Tibetan Buddhists, most assume that they already know the teachings of Christianity and believe it to be inferior to Buddhism.

   a. In fact, they usually have an understanding of the Gospel that has been distorted by Western culture.

   b. If it is at all possible, give them a copy (perhaps a red-letter edition) of the New Testament and encourage them to read the words of Jesus. If they are truly searching for the truth, the Holy Spirit will open their eyes when they read and consider the words of Christ.

Part IV:
Selected Bibliography

I. Primary Sources of Far Eastern Religions

A. Buddhist Scriptures

Bardo Thodol.

> The Tibetan Book of the Dead is a famous Tibetan scripture that describes the forty-nine-day period between death and rebirth.

Conze, Edward, I. B. Horner, David Snellgrove, and Arthur Waley, eds. *Buddhist Texts through the Ages.* New York: Harper & Row, 1954.

> This book offers an English translation of key passages from the sacred literature of the major schools of Buddhism, including Pali, Sanskrit, Chinese, Tibetan, and Japanese texts.

Kangyur.

> Sacred scriptures of Tibetan Buddhism.

Lotus Sutra.

> This Sanskrit work, along with other Sanskrit sutras, is sacred to Mahayana Buddhists.

Tripitaka, or the Pali Canon.

> This Buddhist scripture is the most complete and generally regarded as the earliest collection of canonical literature in Buddhism. It was written in the Pali language and is sacred to Theravadin Buddhists.

B. Taoist Thought

Tao Te Ching.

> This text contains eighty-one brief poems supposedly composed by Lao Tzu.

Chuang Tzu.

> The second most important document in Taoism, this text articulates the soundness of Taoist philosophy.

C. Confucian Canon

1. The Five Classics include the books of Poetry, History, Changes, Rites, and the Annals of Spring and Autumn.

   The famous *I Ching* (the book of changes) is a handbook on divination and became one of the Classics several centuries after the life of Confucius.

2. The Four Books include *Analects, Mencius, Great Learning,* and *Doctrine of the Mean.*

   The *Analects* is a collection of well-known sayings supposedly written by Confucius.

II. Secondary Sources of Far Eastern Religions

A. Major Comprehensive Works

Creel, H. G. *Chinese Thought from Confucius to Mao Tse-tung.* New York: Mentor, 1953.

Despite its age and brevity, this book provides an excellent understanding of the development of Confucianism, Taoism, and Buddhism in China.

Crim, Keith, ed. *The Perennial Dictionary of World Religions.* San Francisco: Harper & Row, 1989.

This dictionary was originally published as the *Abingdon Dictionary of Living Religions* (1981). It is an outstanding reference source that clearly and accurately defines all the basic concepts of the Far Eastern Religions.

Noss, John B. *Man's Religions.* 2d ed. New York: Macmillan, 1956.

This standard reference book covers the history of all the major religions and many of the minor ones as well.

B. Major Works on Buddhism

Gyatso, Tenzin. *The World of Tibetan Buddhism.* Boston: Wisdom Publications, 1995.

The Dalai Lama provides his interpretation of the major doctrines of Buddhism and discusses the distinctive features of Vajrayana Buddhism.

Kalupahana, David J. *Buddhist Philosophy: A Historical Analysis.* Honolulu: University Press of Hawaii, 1976.

Though highly technical, this book provides an excellent examination of the major philosophies of early Buddhism.

Layman, Emma McCloy. *Buddhism in America.* Chicago: Nelson-Hall, 1976.

This book offers a good survey of how the major schools of Buddhism became established in North America.

Rahula, Walpola. *What the Buddha Taught.* New York: Grove Press, 1974.

This book analyzes the Four Noble Truths and the Buddhist doctrine of no soul. It is unrivaled for a basic and clear understanding of the teachings of the Buddha from a Buddhist perspective.

Saunders, E. Dale. *Buddhism in Japan with an Outline of Its Origins in India.* Philadelphia: University of Pennsylvania Press, 1971.

This book traces many of the Mahayana branches of Buddhism from India to China and finally to Japan.

Snellgrove, David, and Hugh Richardson. *A Cultural History of Tibet.* Boulder, Colo.: Prajna Press, 1980.

An excellent presentation of how Buddhism historically was incorporated into the Tibetan culture.

Thomas, Edward J. *The Life of Buddha as Legend and History.* London: Routledge & Kegan Paul, 1975.

This book provides the finest authoritative account of all that is known of the life of the Buddha.

III. Christian Critiques of Far Eastern Religions

A. Major Books

Anderson, J. N. D. *Christianity and Comparative Religion.* Downers Grove, Ill.: InterVarsity Press, 1970.

This classic book examines how the major religions view God, including the views of Theravada and Mahayana Buddhism. Highly technical, it focuses only on doctrinal issues.

Johnson, David L. *A Reasoned Look at Asian Religions.* Minneapolis: Bethany House, 1985.

This book briefly discusses fundamental doctrines of most of the major world religions, including Buddhism, Taoism, and Confucianism. It offers astute insights into the differences between these religions and Christianity.

Mather, George A., and Larry A. Nichols. *Dictionary of Cults, Sects, Religions and the Occult.* Grand Rapids: Zondervan, 1993.

This dictionary contains many exceptional articles on all the religions discussed in this book. It is the finest dictionary written by Christians on this area of study.

Neill, Stephen. *Christian Faith and Other Religions.* London: Oxford University Press, 1970.

This book provides penetrating comparisons between the Buddha and Christ. Although the book is not strong on Buddhist philosophy, it offers a lucid portrayal of these two figures.

Yamamoto, J. Isamu. *Beyond Buddhism: A Basic Introduction to the Buddhist Tradition.* Downers Grove, Ill.: InterVarsity Press, 1982.

A helpful and accurate introduction to the Buddhist religion. It provides a brief history of this religion, a basic understanding of its major doctrines, and a Christian response.

B. Major Journals

Short, Stephen H. "Zen and the Art of Not Knowing God." *Christian Research Journal* (Winter/Spring 1990).

85

Weldon, John. "Nichiren Shoshu Buddhism." *Christian Research Journal* (Fall 1992).

Yamamoto, J. Isamu. "The Arrival of Theravada: Southeast Asians Bring Their School of Buddhism to America." *Christian Research Journal* (Fall 1994).

_____. "The Buddha and What He Taught." *Christian Research Journal* (Spring/Summer 1994).

_____. "Tibetan Buddhists: Exiled from Their Homeland, Extolled in the West." *Christian Research Journal* (Spring 1995).

_____. "Sharing Your Faith with Asian Americans." *Christian Research Journal* (Summer 1992; Fall 1992; Winter 1993).

_____. "Zest for Zen: North Americans Adopt This Meditative School of Buddhism." *Christian Research Journal* (Winter 1995).

International Journal of Frontier Missions 10, no. 3 (July 1993).

This journal is published by the International Student Leaders Coalition for Frontier Missions. This issue is devoted entirely to evangelism of Buddhists. It is one of the most informative resources on how to reach Buddhists internationally and in North America with the Gospel.

Part V:
Parallel Comparison Chart

Buddhism, Taoism . . .	The Bible

Human Suffering

"This is the noble truth of sorrow. Birth is sorrow, age is sorrow, disease is sorrow, death is sorrow. . . . in short, all the five components of individuality is sorrow" (*Samyutta-nikaya* 5:4; from the Pali Canon).

"To one who is thus not wisely reflecting, one of six speculative views may arise as though it were real and true: 'there is self for me.' . . . fettered by this fetter, the ordinary uninstructed person is not freed from birth, from aging and dying or from grief, sorrow, suffering, lamentation and despair. I say that he is not freed from suffering" (*Majjhima-Nikaya* I, 8).

"While realizing that there is no permanent or immutable entity called the 'self,' [the Buddha] also found that belief in such an entity led to further suffering. Belief in a permanent entity such as the *atman* often led to selfishness and egoism. This, for him, was the root cause of craving and its attendant suffering" (David J. Kalupahana, *Buddhist Philosophy*, 38).

Jesus said, "You will grieve, but your grief will turn to joy. . . . Now is your time of grief, but I will see you again and you will rejoice, and no one will take away your joy" (John 16:20, 22).

Jesus then said, "I have told you these things, so that in me you may have peace. In this world you will have trouble. But take heart! I have overcome the world" (John 16:33).

"Dear friends, do not be surprised at the painful trial you are suffering, as though something strange were happening to you. But rejoice that you participate in the sufferings of Christ, so that you may be overjoyed when his glory is revealed. If you are insulted because of the name of Christ, you are blessed, for the Spirit of glory and of God rests on you. If you suffer, it should not be as a murderer or thief or any other kind of criminal, or even as a meddler. However, if you suffer as a Christian, do not be ashamed, but praise God that you bear that name" (1 Peter 4:12–16).

The Human Soul

"Persons are a conglomeration of skandhas, elements and sense-fields, devoid of a self or anything belonging to a self. Consciousness arises from ignorance, karma and craving, and it keeps going by settling down in the grasping at form" (*Lanleavatara Sutra,* 68).

"Buddhism stands unique in the history of human thought in denying the existence of such a Soul, Self, or *Atman.* According to the teaching of the Buddha, the idea of self is an imaginary, false belief which has no corresponding reality, and it produces harmful thoughts of 'me' and 'mine,' selfish desire, craving, attachment, hatred, ill-will, conceit, pride, egoism, and other defilements, impurities, and problems" (Walpola Rahula, *What the Buddha Taught,* 51).

The Buddha taught, "I had no notion of a self, or of a being, or of a soul, or of a person, nor had I any notion or non-notion" (*Vajracchedika,* 14).

"Nirvana is definitely no annihilation of self, because there is no self to annihilate.... An Arahant [Buddhist saint] after his death is often compared to a fire gone out when the supply of wood is over, or to the flame of a lamp gone out when the wick and oil are finished. Here it should be clearly and distinctly understood, without any confusion, that what is compared to a flame or a fire gone out is *not* Nirvana, but the 'being' composed of the Five Aggregates who realized Nirvana" (Walpola Rahula, *What the Buddha Taught,* 37, 41–42).

"As the deer pants for streams of water, so my soul pants for you, O God. My soul thirsts for God, for the living God" (Ps. 42:1–2).

"Find rest, O my soul, in God alone" (Ps. 62:5).

"The LORD is my shepherd, I shall lack nothing.... he restores my soul" (Ps. 23:1, 3).

"But the things that come out of the mouth come from the heart, and these make a man 'unclean.' For out of the heart come evil thoughts, murder, adultery, sexual immorality, theft, false testimony, slander" (Matt. 15:18–19).

"Hear, O Israel: The LORD our God, the LORD is one. Love the LORD your God with all your heart and with all you soul and with all your strength" (Deut. 6:4–5).

"Jesus replied: ' "Love the Lord your God with all your heart and with all your soul and with all your mind." This is the first and greatest commandment'" (Matt. 22:37–38).

"Keep yourselves in God's love as you wait for the mercy of our Lord Jesus Christ to bring you to eternal life" (Jude 21).

"The gift of God is eternal life in Christ Jesus our Lord" (Rom. 6:23).

Jesus said, "My sheep listen to my voice; I know them, and they follow me. I give them eternal life, and they shall never perish" (John 10:27–28a).

"God has given us eternal life, and this life is in his Son" (1 John 5:11).

Emptiness

"Impermanent and unstable are all conditioned things" (*Lalitavistara.* XIII, 95).

"So one who is convinced of the emptiness of everything has no likes or dislikes. For he knows that that which he might like is just empty, and he sees it as just empty" (*Sikshasamuccaya, 264*).

"Regard the world as void" (*Suttanipata,* 119).

Jesus Christ is the same yesterday and today and forever" (Heb. 13:8).

The Lord says, "so is my word that goes out from my mouth: It will not return to me empty, but will accomplish what I desire and achieve the purpose for which I sent it" (Isa. 55:11).

Jesus Christ "who descended is the very one who ascended higher than all the heavens, in order to fill the whole universe" (Eph. 4:10).

Salvation

"Be lamps unto yourselves. Be a refuge unto yourselves. Do not turn to any external refuge.... Work out your own salvation with diligence" (*Mahaparinibbana-sutta* 2:33; 6:10; from the Pali Canon).

"A Bodhisattva resolves: I take upon myself the burden of all suffering" (*Sikshasamuccaya,* 280 [Mahayana Buddhism]).

"For it is by grace you have been saved, through faith—and this not from yourselves, it is the gift of God—not by works, so that no one can boast" (Eph. 2:8–9).

"Surely [Jesus Christ] took up our infirmities and carried our sorrows.... he was crushed for our iniquities; the punishment that brought us peace was upon him, and by his wounds we are healed. We all, like sheep, have gone astray, each of us has turned to his own way; and the LORD has laid on him the iniquity of us all" (Isa. 53:4–6).

Salvation, cont.

"We have one who speaks to the Father in our defense—Jesus Christ, the Righteous One. He is the atoning sacrifice for our sins, and not only for ours but also for the sins of the whole world" (1 John 2:1–2).

"Amitabha, the Protector . . . endowed with great compassion, created for the world's saving" (*Aryatarabhattarikanamashtottarasatakastotra,* 12–13 [Amida Buddhism]).

"Because Jesus lives forever, he has a permanent priesthood. Therefore he is able to save completely those who come to God through him, because he always lives to intercede for them. Such a high priest meets our need—one who is holy, blameless, pure, set apart from sinners, exalted above the heavens" (Heb. 7:24–26).

"And when you're in the company of your master, do not look for faults and virtues, good and bad. If you do, you'll see him as a mass of faults. Just practise clarity of mind and exert yourselves" (Milarepa, *mGur-h Bum* [Tibetan Buddhism]).

"Dear friends, do not believe every spirit, but test the spirits to see whether they are from God, because many false prophets have gone out into the world. This is how you can recognize the Spirit of God: Every spirit that acknowledges that Jesus Christ has come in the flesh is from God, but every spirit that does not acknowledge Jesus is not from God" (1 John 4:1–3).

"What you do not want done to yourself, do not do to others" (Confucius, *Analects,* 15:23).

"See to it that no one takes you captive through hollow and deceptive philosophy, which depends on human tradition and the basic principles of this world rather than on Christ. For in Christ all the fullness of the Deity lives in bodily form" (Col. 2:8–9).

Jesus said, "In everything, do to others what you would have them do to you" (Matt. 7:12; see also Luke 6:31).

God

"Yet you [the Buddha] preach compassion for all beings, O you God above the Gods! ... Let us therefore worship you, the chief and best of men, worthy of our worship" (*Sikshasamuccaya,* 259 [Mahayana Buddhism]).

"To go to him [the Buddha] for refuge, to praise and to honour him, to abide in his religion, that is fit for those with sense. The only Protector, he is without faults or their residues; the All-knowing, he has all the virtues, and that without fail" (*Matrceta, Satapancasatkastotra,* I, 2–3).

"By the enjoyment of all desires, to which one devotes oneself just as one pleases, it is by such practice as this that one may speedily gain Buddhahood. With the enjoyment of all desires, to which one devotes oneself just as one pleases, in union with one's chosen divinity, one worships oneself, the Supreme One" (*Guhyasamajatantra,* ch. 7 [Tibetan Buddhism]).

"And God spoke all these words: 'I am the LORD your God.... You shall have no other gods before me.... You shall not bow down to them or worship them; for I, the LORD your God, am a jealous God" (Ex. 20:1–3, 5).

"The LORD is gracious and righteous; our God is full of compassion" (Ps. 116:5).

"Therefore God exalted him to the highest place and gave him the name that is above every name, that at the name of Jesus every knee should bow, in heaven and on earth and under the earth, and every tongue confess that Jesus Christ is Lord, to the glory of God the Father" (Phil. 2:9–11).

"The eternal God is your refuge" (Deut. 33:27).

God says about his Son Jesus Christ, "You have loved righteousness and hated wickedness; therefore God, your God, has set you above your companions" (Heb. 1:9).

In addition, the apostle Peter called Jesus, "the Holy and Righteous One" (Acts 3:14).

"The wrath of God is being revealed from heaven against all the godlessness and wickedness of men who suppress the truth by their wickedness, since what may be known about God is plain to them, because God has made it plain to them. For since the creation of the world God's invisible qualities—his eternal power and divine nature—have been clearly seen,

91

God, cont.

being understood from what has been made, so that men are without excuse.

"For although they knew God, they neither glorified him as God nor gave thanks to him, but their thinking became futile and their foolish hearts were darkened. Although they claimed to be wise, they became fools and exchanged the glory of the immortal God for images made to look like mortal man and birds and animals and reptiles.

"Therefore God gave them over in the sinful desires of their hearts to sexual impurity for the degrading of their bodies with one another. They exchanged the truth of God for a lie, and worshiped and served created things rather than the Creator—who is forever praised. Amen" (Rom. 1:18–25).

"For whoever exalts himself will be humbled" (Matt. 23:12; Luke 14:11; 18:14).

"The Nameless is the origin of Heaven and Earth" (*The Way of Lao-tzu,* 1).

God told Moses to tell the Israelites that his name is "I am who I am. . . . This is my name forever, the name by which I am to be remembered from generation to generation" (Ex. 3:14–15).

"All things in the world come from being. And being comes from nonbeing" (*The Way of Lao-tzu,* 40).

"In the beginning God created the heavens and the earth" (Gen. 1:1).

"Through him [Jesus] all things were made; without him nothing was made that has been made" (John 1:3).

 # Part VI: *Glossary*

When two entries are given, the first entry is in Sanskrit and the second in parenthesis is in Pali. Note that in the text a word might be either Sanskrit or Pali, depending on whether the focus is Theravada (Pali) or Mahayana (usually Sanskrit).

Abhidharma (Abhidhamma)	Analysis of the philosophy and psychology of Buddhism. It is the third and historically the latest of the three sections (or "baskets") of the Pali Canon.
Ajari	A spiritual master adept in ascetic practices in the Shugendo sect of Japanese Buddhism.
Amidism	Salvation by faith in the compassion of Amida Buddha.
Anatman (Anatta)	The Buddhist doctrine of no-soul.
Anitya (Anicca)	The impermanence of all things.
Arahant, Arhan (Arhant, Arhat)	A person in Theravada Buddhism who has perfected the Four Noble Truths in Buddhist philosophy.
Bodhisattva (Bodhisatta)	A being who seeks enlightenment but delays Buddhahood in order to save others by his own merits.
Buddha	A person who has experienced enlightenment, or specifically Siddhartha Gautama, the founder of Buddhism.
Butsu-dan	A portable Buddhist shrine in the homes of Buddhists. A place where the family worships and brings offerings, such as fruit, flowers, and rice.
Chun Tzu	The Chinese ideal of a gentleman.
Daikyo	"Great Doctrine."
Dharma (Dhamma)	The natural order of the world, society, and life. Indian religions defined this term according to their own ethics, religious duty, and view of righteousness. In Buddhism, Dharma is particularly significant as it is referred to as the doctrine of the Buddha.
Dharmakaya	The Universal Buddha.

Duhka (Dukkha)	All forms of suffering. It is the First Noble Truth of Buddhism.
Eightfold Path	The fourth of the Four Noble Truths, which comprise the Buddhist ethics.
Enlightenment	The revelation of Absolute Truth.
Gohonzon	A small Buddhist altar prevalent in Nichiren Buddhism.
Hinayana	Literally, "the little or lesser vehicle." To the Theravadists it is a disparaging term.
I Ching	"The Book of Changes," which deals with methods of divination.
Jiriki	The way of salvation by self-effort in the Japanese schools of Buddhism, such as Zen Buddhism.
Kami-no-michi	"Way of the Gods."
Karma (Kamma)	The law of cause and effect; a doctrine that a person's actions of the past, including past lives, govern the present life, and that past and present actions govern future lives.
Kensho	The term for "enlightenment" in Zen Buddhism.
Koan	A statement that cannot be resolved or understood by the intellect in order to cut through the rational process of the mind to achieve enlightenment.
Lama	A priest or monk teacher in Tibetan Buddhism.
Magga	The path that leads to cessation of suffering. It is the Fourth Noble Truth of Buddhism, and is known as the "Middle Path."
Mandala	In Buddhism, a mythical representation of the cosmic universe with the Buddha at the center and other figures surrounding him.
Mantras	The verbal formulas employed to effect spiritual power.
"Middle Way"	The way to truth, which averts both worldly pleasures and extreme austerities.
Mondo	The rapid exchange between master and disciple in order to attain enlightenment of the disciple in Zen Buddhism.
Mudra	The bodily gestures that accompany meditation, particularly hand and finger positions.
Nirmanakaya	The historical Buddha.

Nirodha The termination of suffering. It is known as the Third Noble Truth of suffering.

Nirvana (Nibbana) Literally, the "void"; the attainment of enlightenment during life; the annihilation of the impermanent elements that constitute a being at death.

Parinirvana Liberation from the cycle of rebirth or extinction.

Pativedhanana The Four Noble Truths, which discuss the universality of suffering, the cause of suffering, the annihilation of suffering, and the Eightfold Path.

Prajna The female, passive principle, expressed in terms of "wisdom."

Prayer wheel (Mani-cho-khor) A cylinder containing Buddhist scriptures, which serves as an aid in meditation, symbolizing the turning of the wheel of the Dharma.

Roshi A Zen master.

Sambbhogakaya The eternal Buddha or the Buddha ideal.

Samgha (Sangha) Specifically, the Buddhist monastic order; generally, the society of Buddhist believers.

Samsara Literally, "wheel-turning"; the continuous round of death and rebirth.

Samudaya The origin of suffering. It is the Second Noble Truth of Buddhism.

Sanzen Instructive dialogue between the Zen master and student.

Satori The state of enlightenment in Zen Buddhism.

Shaktism The Indian religion in which duality is divided into male and female elements, such as power, deities, and sexuality.

Shamanism A belief in good and evil spirits who can be influenced by a priest or medicine man, known as a shaman.

Shinto "Way of the Gods."

Shunyata The Void or emptiness.

Sutras (Suttas) Sermons or discourses that have become Buddhist scriptures.

Tanha The grasping, craving, or attachment to things leading to suffering. Some Buddhists refer to it as the Second Noble Truth of Buddhism.

95

Tantrism	The mystical nature of esoteric Buddhism, using such techniques as mantras, yantras, and mudras.
Tao	A concept with complex meanings not definable in words for the Chinese, but generally known as "the Way."
Tao De Ching	"The Book of the Virtuous Way."
Tariki	The way of salvation, not by self-effort, but by the power of an external force in the Japanese schools of Buddhism, such as the Amidist schools.
Theravada	"The Doctrine of the Elders"; the fundamentalist branch of Buddhism; the southern school of Buddhism.
Trikaya	The three manifestations of the Buddha: Nirmanakaya, Sambhogakaya, and Dharmakaya.
Tripitaka (Tipitaka)	The three baskets composed of the Vinaya-pitaka (the rules of the discipline of the Buddhist order), the Sutta-pitaka (sermons of the Buddha), and the Abhidharma (philosophical commentaries on the teachings of the Buddha); the three main divisions of the Pali Canon, the corpus of sacred texts in Buddhism.
Upaya	The male, active principle, expressed in terms of "love and compassion."
Vajrayana	Literally, "the Diamond Vehicle"; the Tantric form of Buddhism, prevalent in Tibet; a derivation of Mahayana Buddhism.
Vinaya	Rules and regulations within the Buddhist order.
Wheel of the Law (Dharma)	Stages in comprehending ultimate reality. Each turn of the Wheel took Buddhism to a higher level of understanding Absolute Truth, with the Buddha effecting the first turn.
Yana	"Vehicle," or the path one takes to achieve enlightenment or nirvana.
Yang	The male, active principle in Taoism.
Yantras	Visual techniques of meditation in which the mandala is of special use.
Yin	The female, passive principle in Taoism.
Zazen	Meditation in a seated position in Zen Buddhism.
Zendos	Zen centers or meditation halls.